BLUEPRINTS

Art Key Stage 1 Copymasters

Ron Adams

Stanley Thornes (Publishers) Ltd

First published in 1993 by:
Stanley Thornes (Publishers) Ltd
Ellenborough House
Wellington Street
CHELTENHAM GL50 1YW

A catalogue record for this book is available from the British Library.

ISBN 0–7487–1624–6

96 97 98 99 00 / 10 9 8 7 6 5 4 3 2

Typeset by Tech-Set, Gateshead, Tyne & Wear
Printed in Great Britain

CONTENTS

v Introduction

Copymasters

1 Mother and child
2 Face shapes
3 Food shapes 1
4 Food shapes 2
5 Elastic machines
6 Bits of faces
7 Proportions
8 Growing up
9 When I'm 64
10 Family embroidery
11 Stained glass
12 Homes 1
13 Homes 2
14 Homes 3
15 Domestic pottery
16 Willow pattern
17 1 cm grid
18 2 cm grid
19 Islamic pattern 1
20 Islamic pattern 2
21 Islamic pattern 3
22 Islamic pattern 4
23 Islamic pattern 5
24 Islamic pattern 6
25 Geometric town
26 Different views
27 Nosey window cleaner
28 Castle as a home
29a House net
29b House net
30 Building materials 1: Big parquet
31 Building materials 2: Small parquet
32 Building materials 3: Large blocks
33 Building materials 4: Small blocks
34 Building materials 5: Large bricks
35 Building materials 6: Small bricks
36 Building materials 7: Large roof tiles
37 Building materials 8: Small roof tiles
38 Indian symbols
39 Rubbings gallery
40 Large weave
41 Small weave
42 Canvas grid
43 Figure shapes
44 Multi-cultural costumes
45 Hats
46 Sandals
47 Clothes shapes 1
48 Clothes shapes 2
49 *The Emperor's New Clothes*
50 Bag pattern
51 Fish shapes 1
52 Fish shapes 2
53 Sea creatures 1
54 Sea creatures 2
55 Simple boat net
56 Wave
57 Animal shapes 1
58 Animal shapes 2
59 Animal shapes 3
60 Fancy letters
61 Sweet bags and cartons
62 Clown
63 My black and white vehicle
64 My fantastic, futuristic, moving machine
65 Journey strip map
66 Lorry net
67 Canal ware stencil 1
68 Canal ware stencil 2
69 Simple alphabet 1
70 Simple alphabet 2
71 Tree of life
72 William Morris 1: Meadow
73 William Morris 2: Flowers
74 William Morris 3: Leaf
75 William Morris 4: Symmetrical animals
76 Seeds template
77 Magnify
78 Tangram
79 Simple head
80 Little dots
81 Big dots
82 Colours I have made
83 Colours and shapes 1
84 Colours and shapes 2
85 Colours and shapes 3
86 Colours that go together
87 Colours that clash
88 Colour spinner
89 Colour rainbow 1
90 Colour rainbow 2
91 Mood painting 1
92 Mood painting 2
93 Cool and warm
94 Finger and glove puppets
95 Shadow puppets
96 I feel, I remember, I see
97 Line drawings of animals and birds
98 Sculpture quiz
99 Nets for solids 1
100 Nets for solids 2
101 Red and black ceramics
102 Tone grid
103 Record assessment sheet

INTRODUCTION

This book contains 103 photocopiable copymasters linked to many of the activities in the Teacher's Resource Book. Where the copymasters are referred to in the text of the Teacher's Resource Book there are instructions on how to use them. They are referred to by number in the Teacher's Resource Book by this symbol: 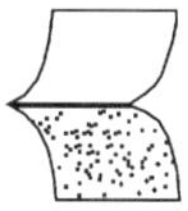 .

The copymasters have two main uses. First to tie directly into the Teacher's Resource Book and provide a core of structured, skill based art activities. Secondly to provide a wide ranging bank of templates, patterns and grid sheets which may be used flexibly beyond the requirements of particular tasks. A Record assessment sheet is also provided. Overall the copymasters are intended to help raise the quality of children's experience of art.

COPYMASTERS 1–103

Mother and child

Draw a blue line around the old pictures.
Colour them all.

Face shapes

How many children in your class

have got round, square, pear or egg

shaped faces?

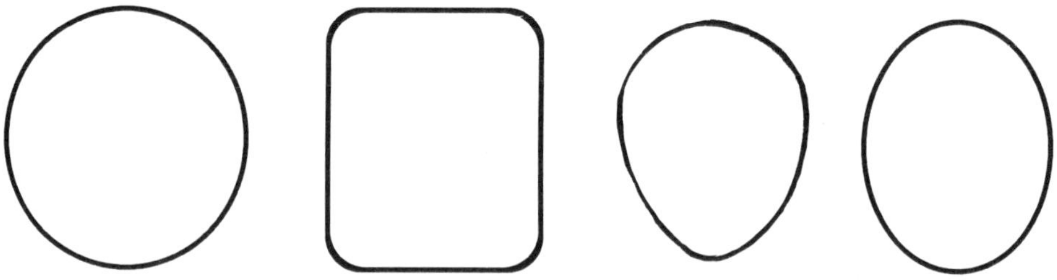

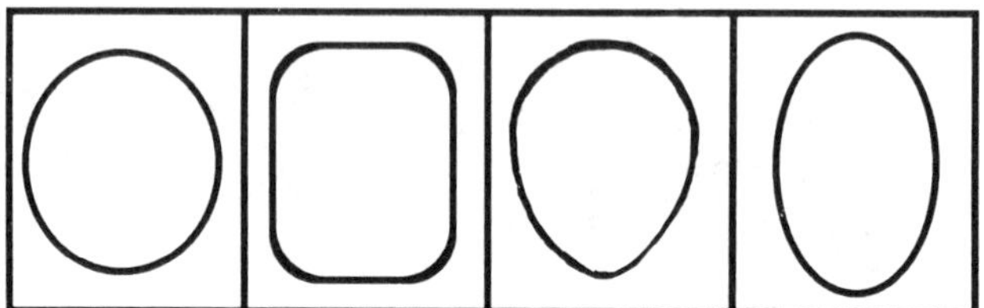

Count them.

This is ________________

He/she has got a

____

face.

Food shapes 1

Cut out and draw around the shapes.

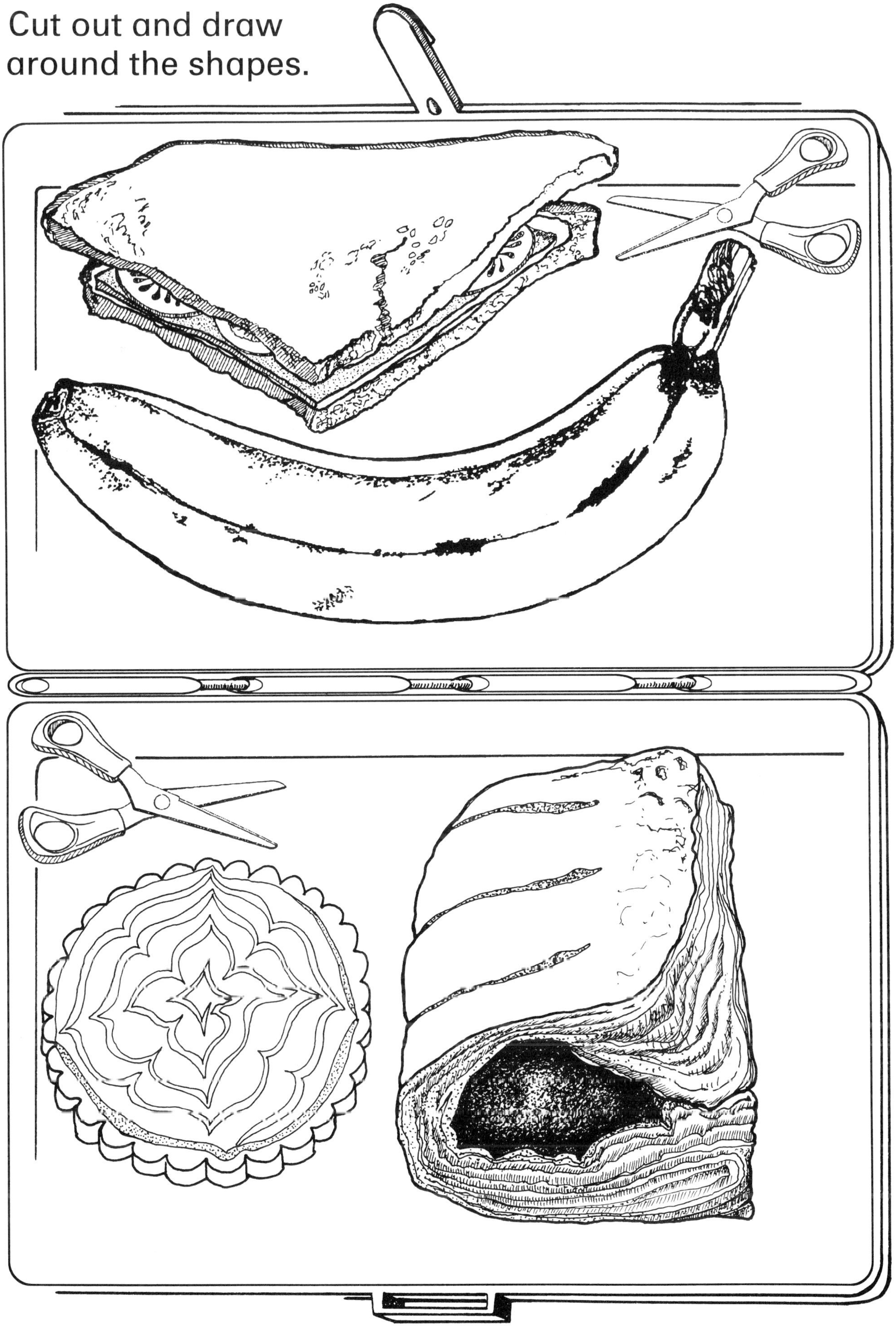

Food shapes 2

Cut out and draw around the shapes.

Elastic machines

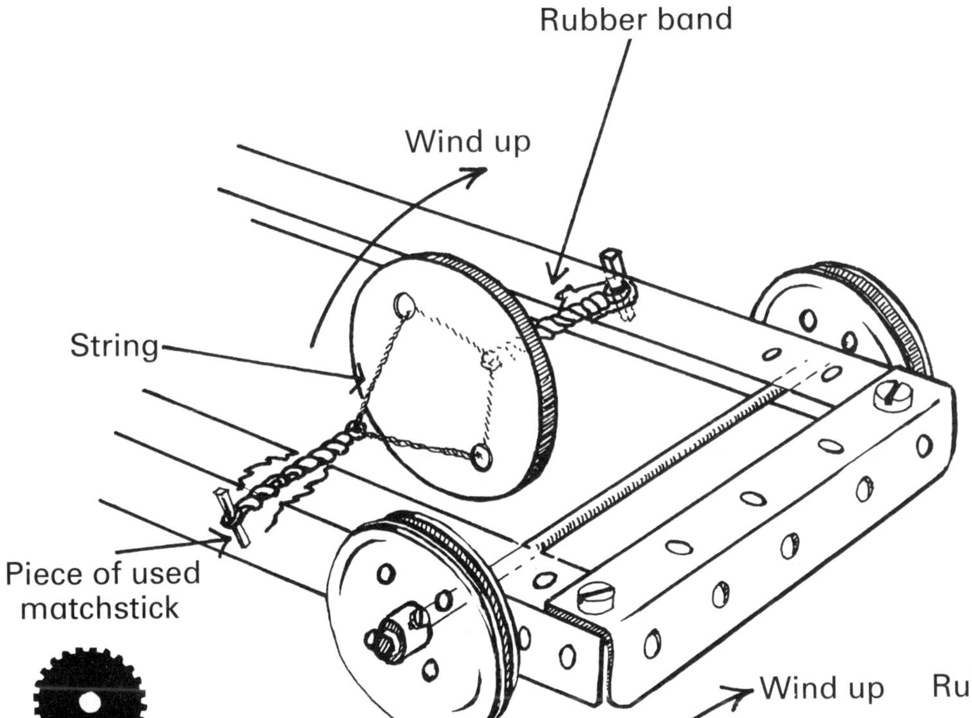

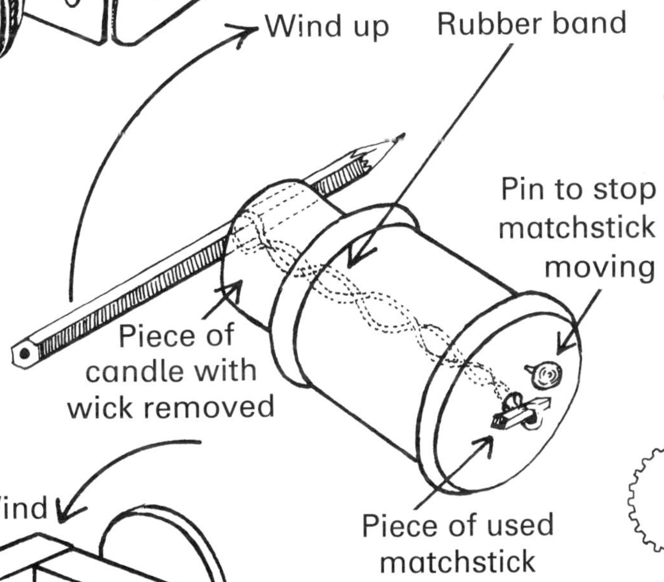

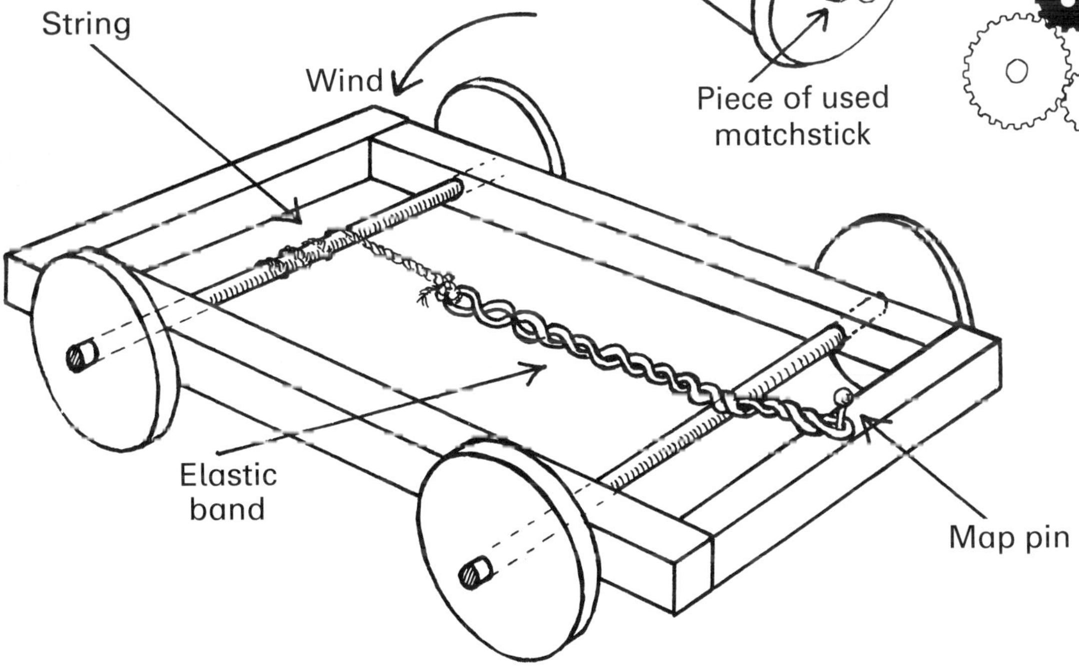

Bits of faces

Features can be all shapes and colours.

My friend is called ______________________________.
Here are her/his

eyes

ear

nose

ear

mouth

Proportions

Look straight at your friend. Where are the eyes, the ears, the nose, the mouth?

Tick your choice.

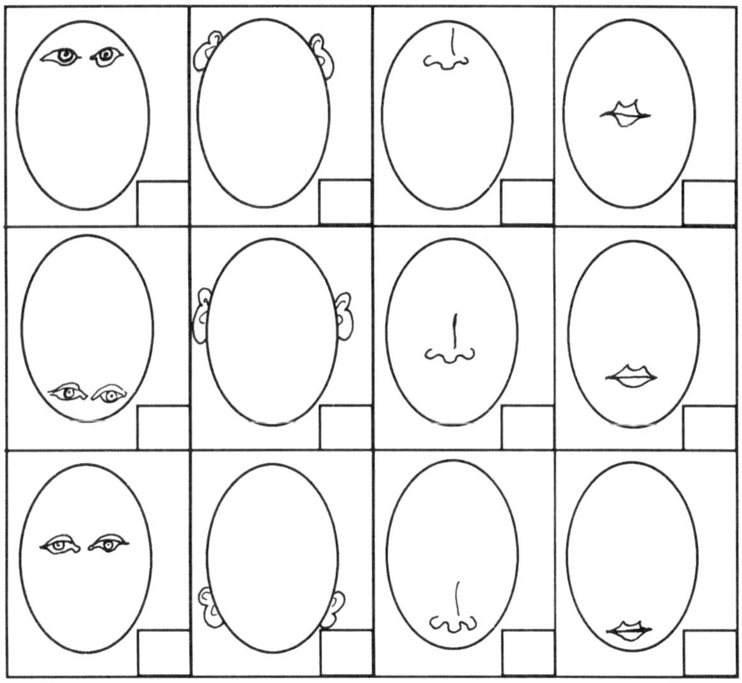

Now carefully draw a picture of your friend in this box.

Growing up

As you grow your body changes. Draw a line from each word to a picture.

When I'm 64

Do four pictures of yourself, as you are now and as you grow older.

Family embroidery

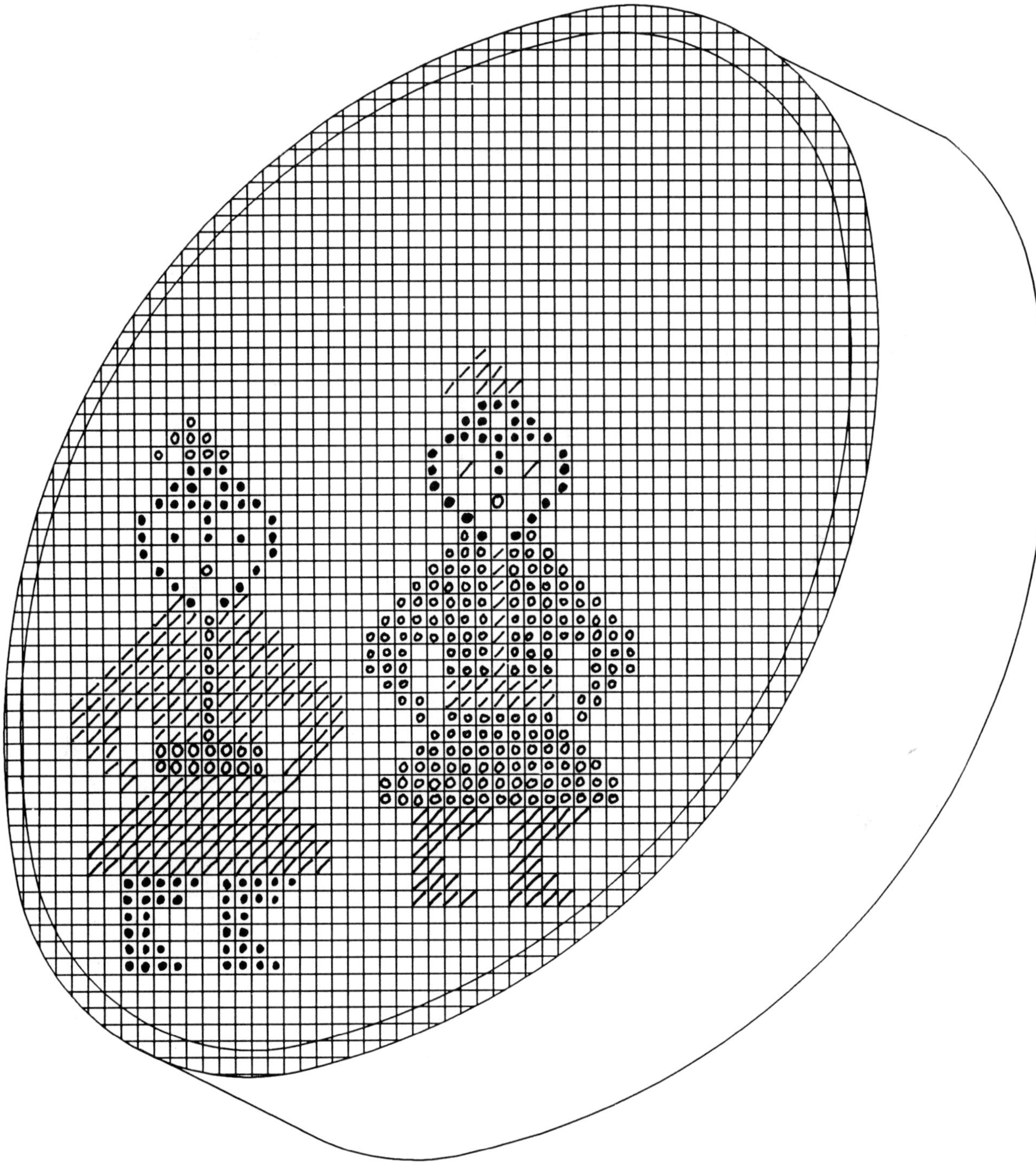

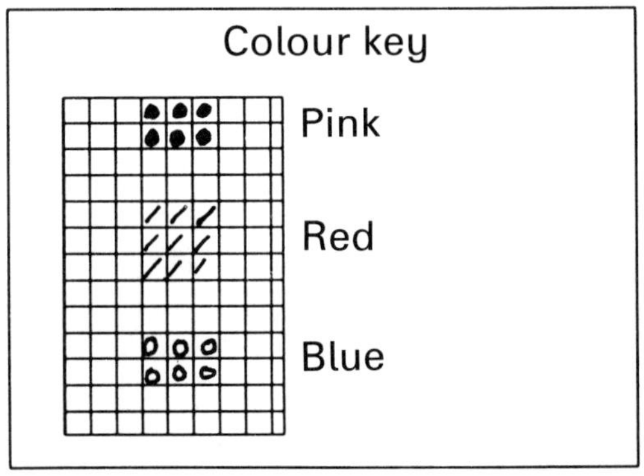

Stained glass

Make your own design. Use black felt tip pen and then colour the shapes.

Homes 1

I have seen a flat.

Here is my picture.

I have seen a terraced house.

Here is my picture.

Homes 2

I have seen a
caravan.

Here is my picture.

I have seen a
thatched cottage.

Here is my picture.

Homes 3

I have seen a castle.

Here is my picture.

I have seen a canal boat.

Here is my picture.

Match the words and pictures. Colour them.

Domestic pottery

Willow pattern

How many trees, birds, people and buildings can you see?
What are the three people on the bridge doing?

1 cm grid

2 cm grid

Islamic pattern 1

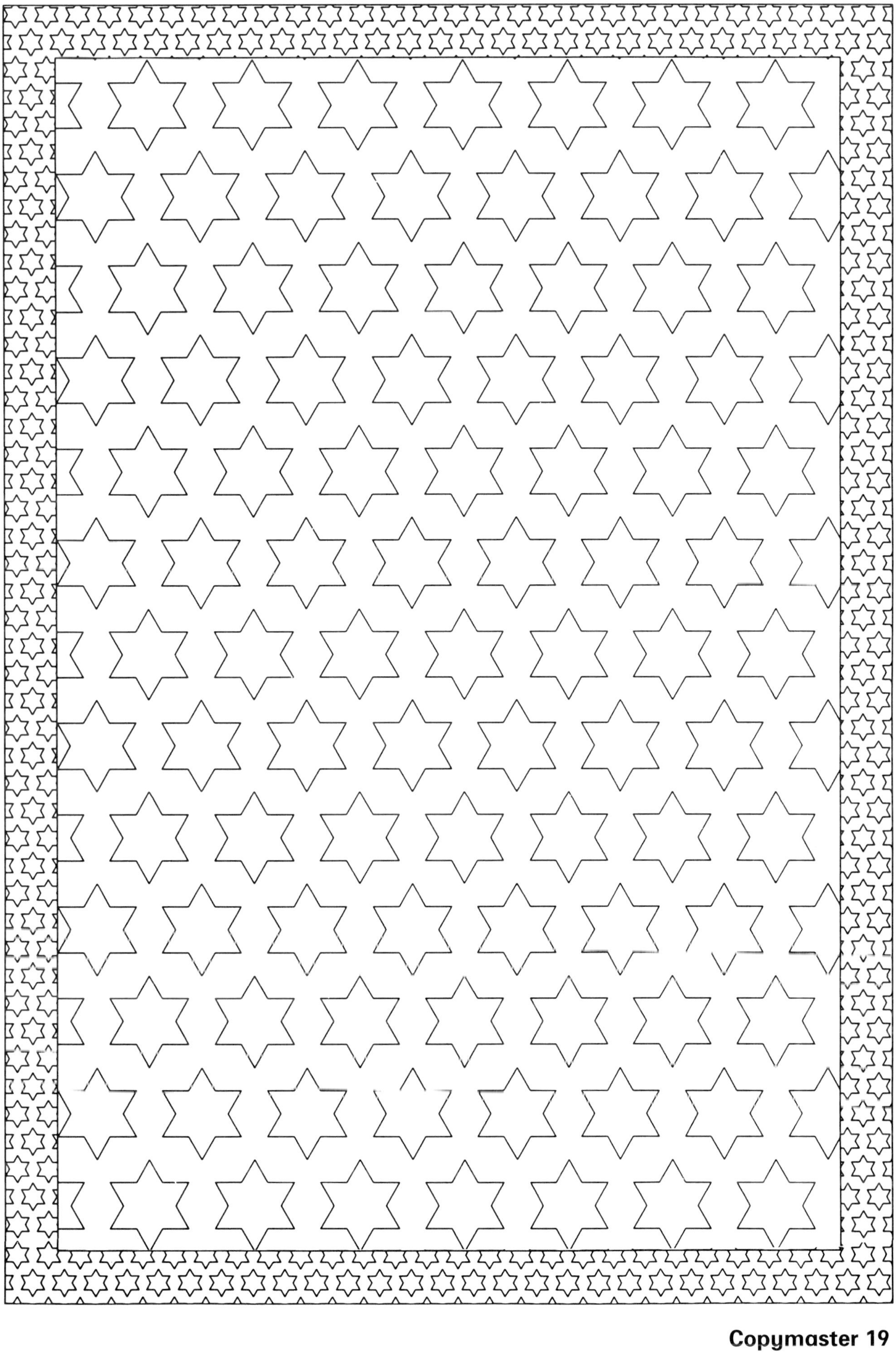

Islamic pattern 2

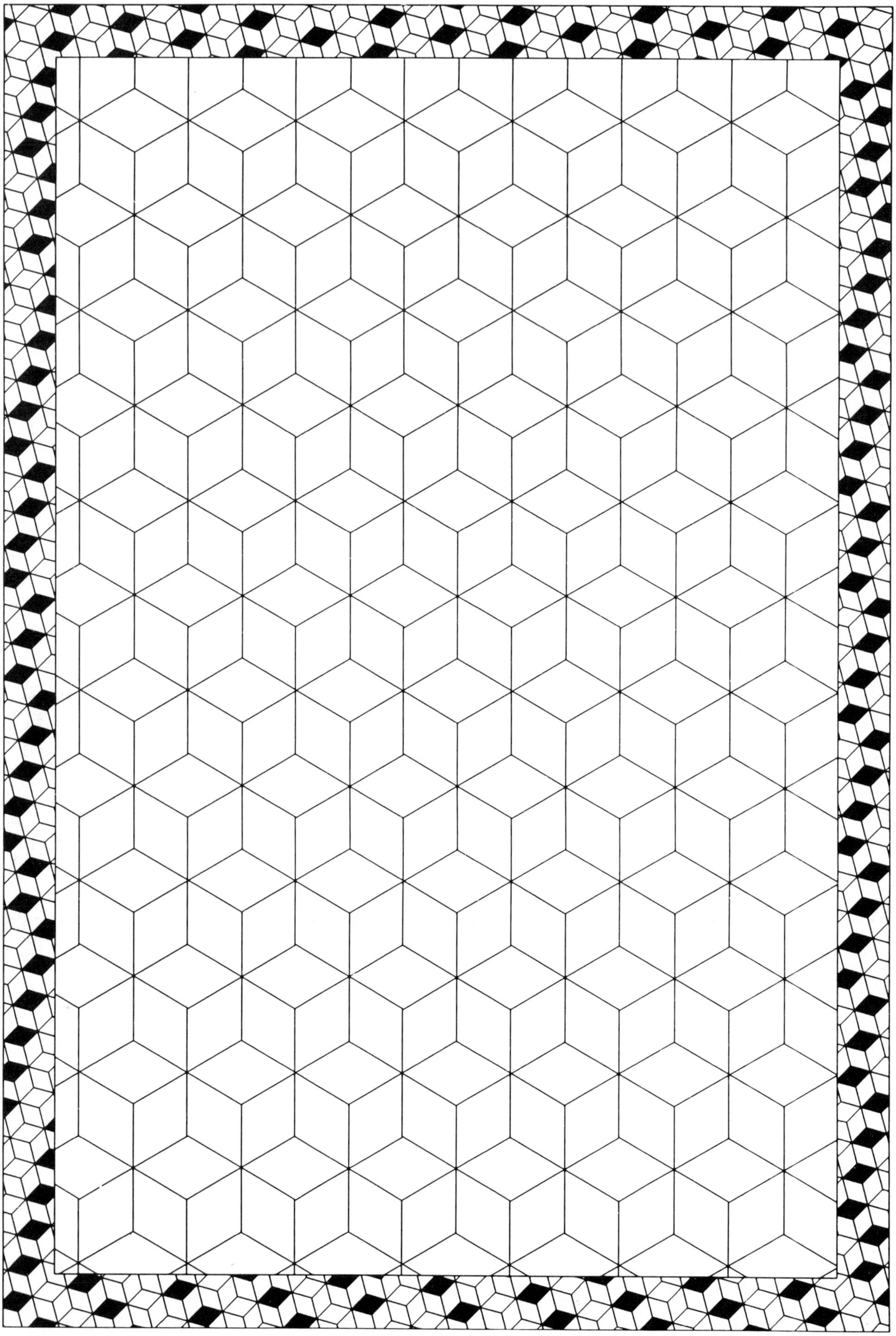

Islamic pattern 3

Islamic pattern 4

Islamic pattern 5

Islamic pattern 6

Geometric town

Different views

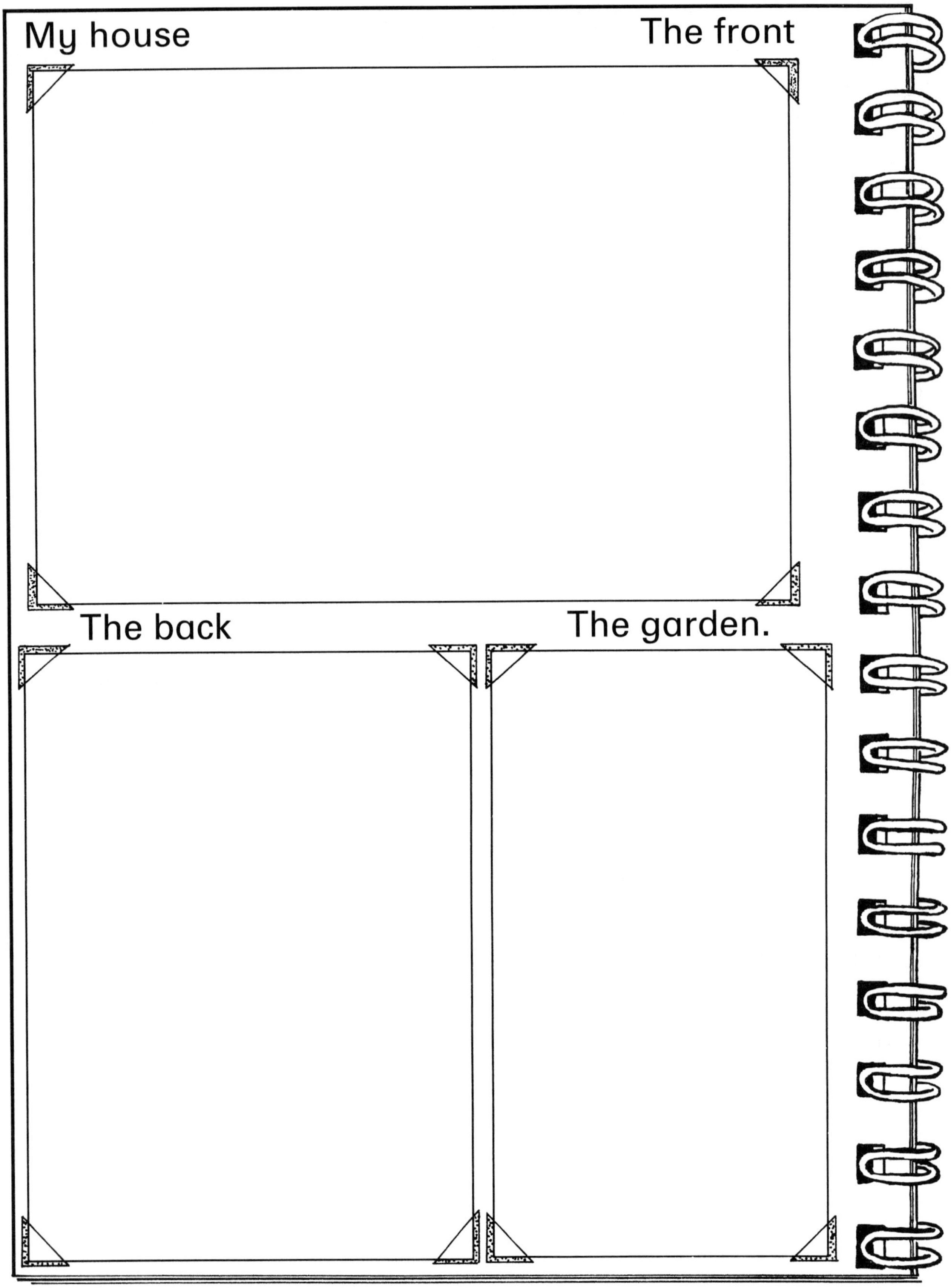

Nosey window cleaner

Castle as a home

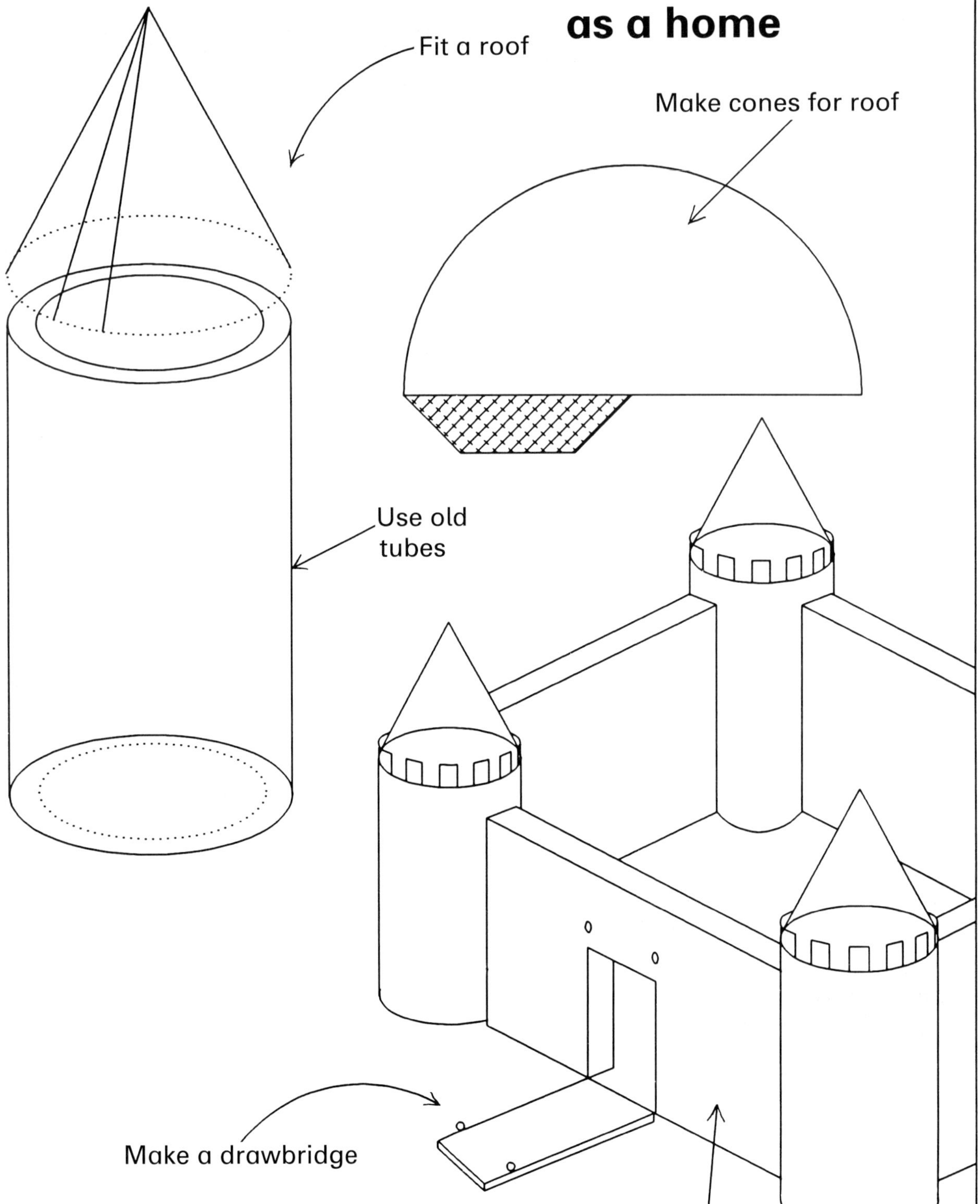

Castles can be made from old boxes, tubes and yogurt pots.

House net (a)

1. Photocopy 29a + 29b onto thin card.
2. Cut out.

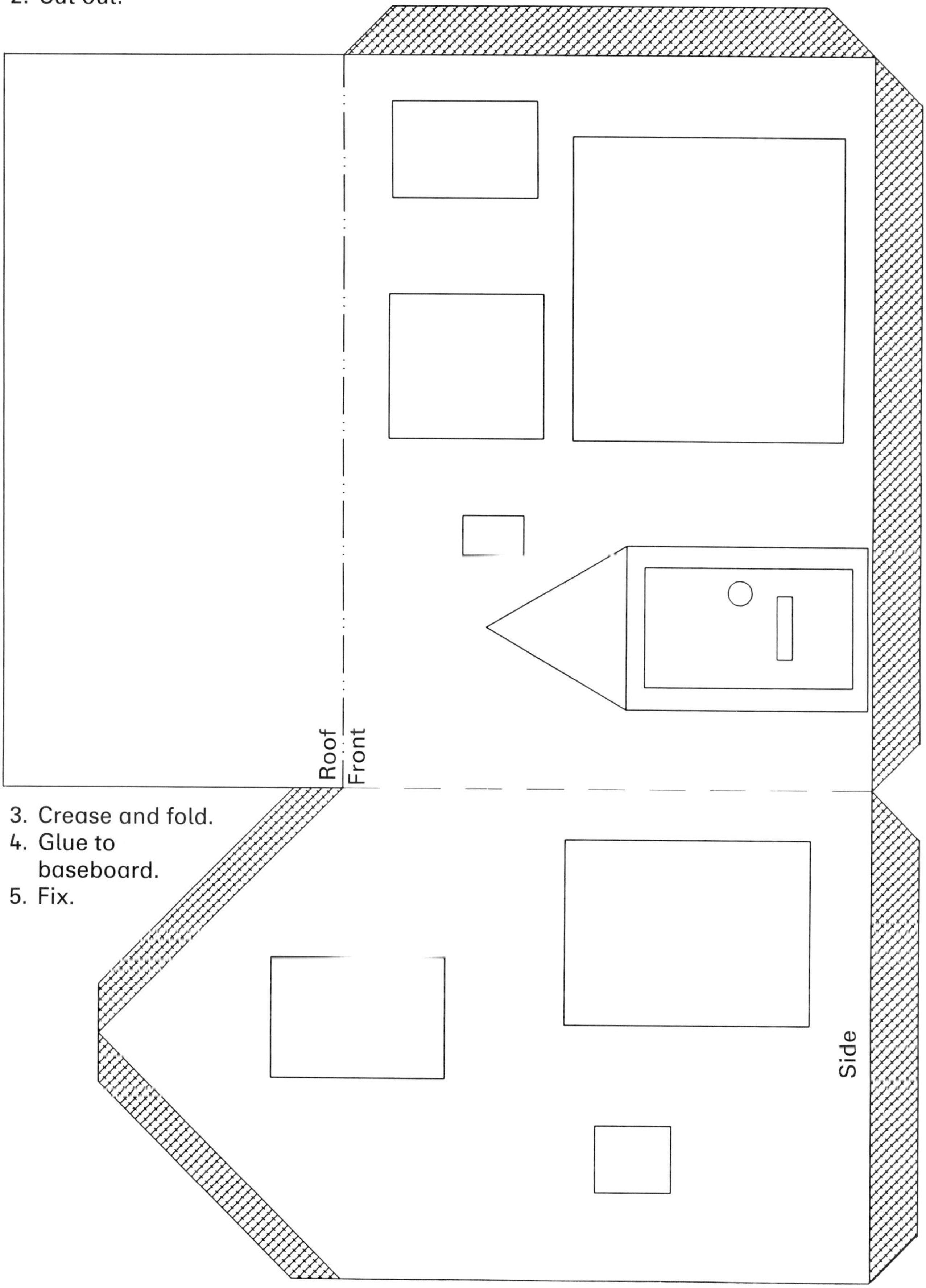

3. Crease and fold.
4. Glue to baseboard.
5. Fix.

House net (b)

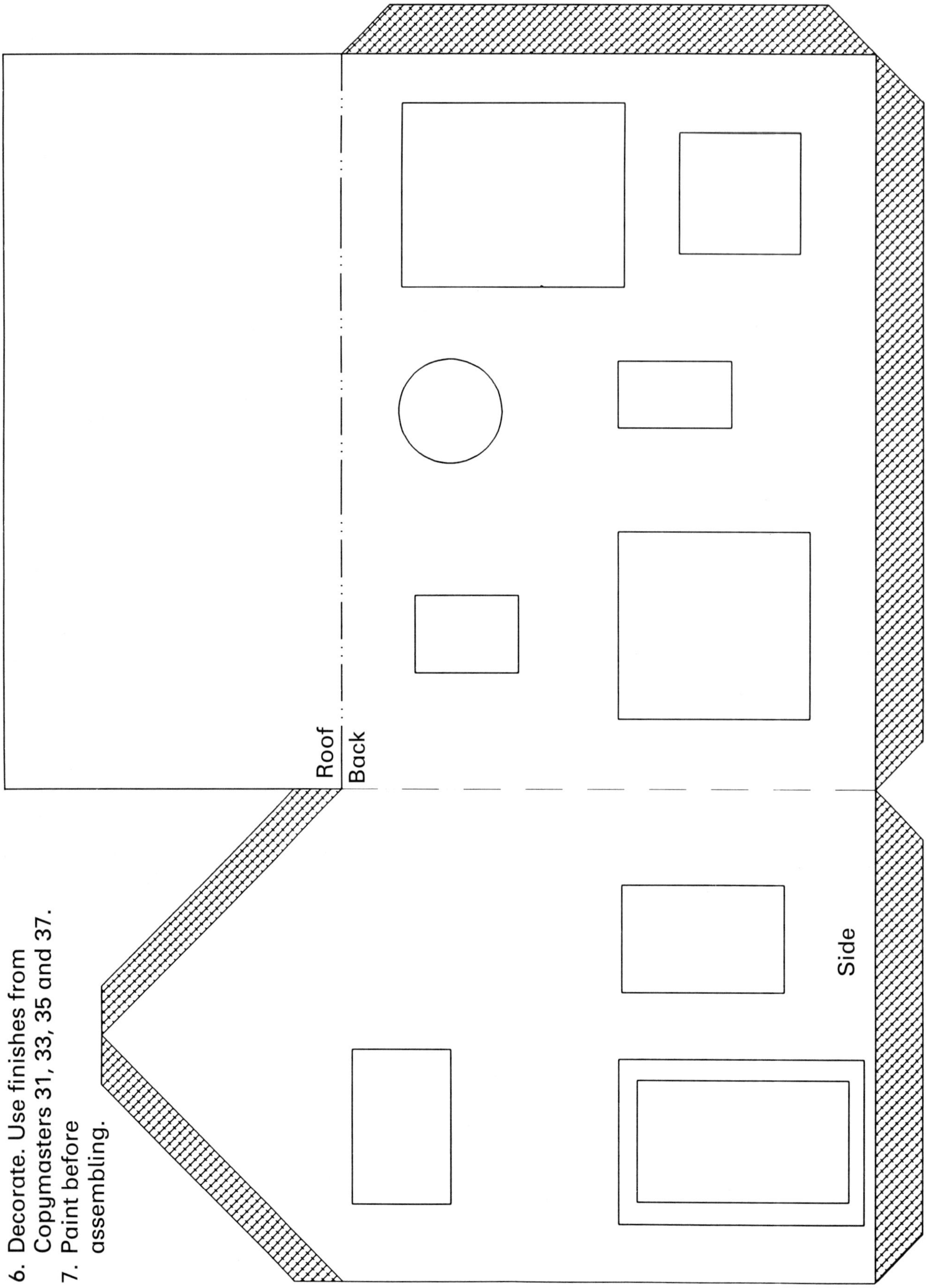

6. Decorate. Use finishes from Copymasters 31, 33, 35 and 37.
7. Paint before assembling.

Building materials 1: Big parquet

Building materials 2: Small parquet

Building materials 3: Large blocks

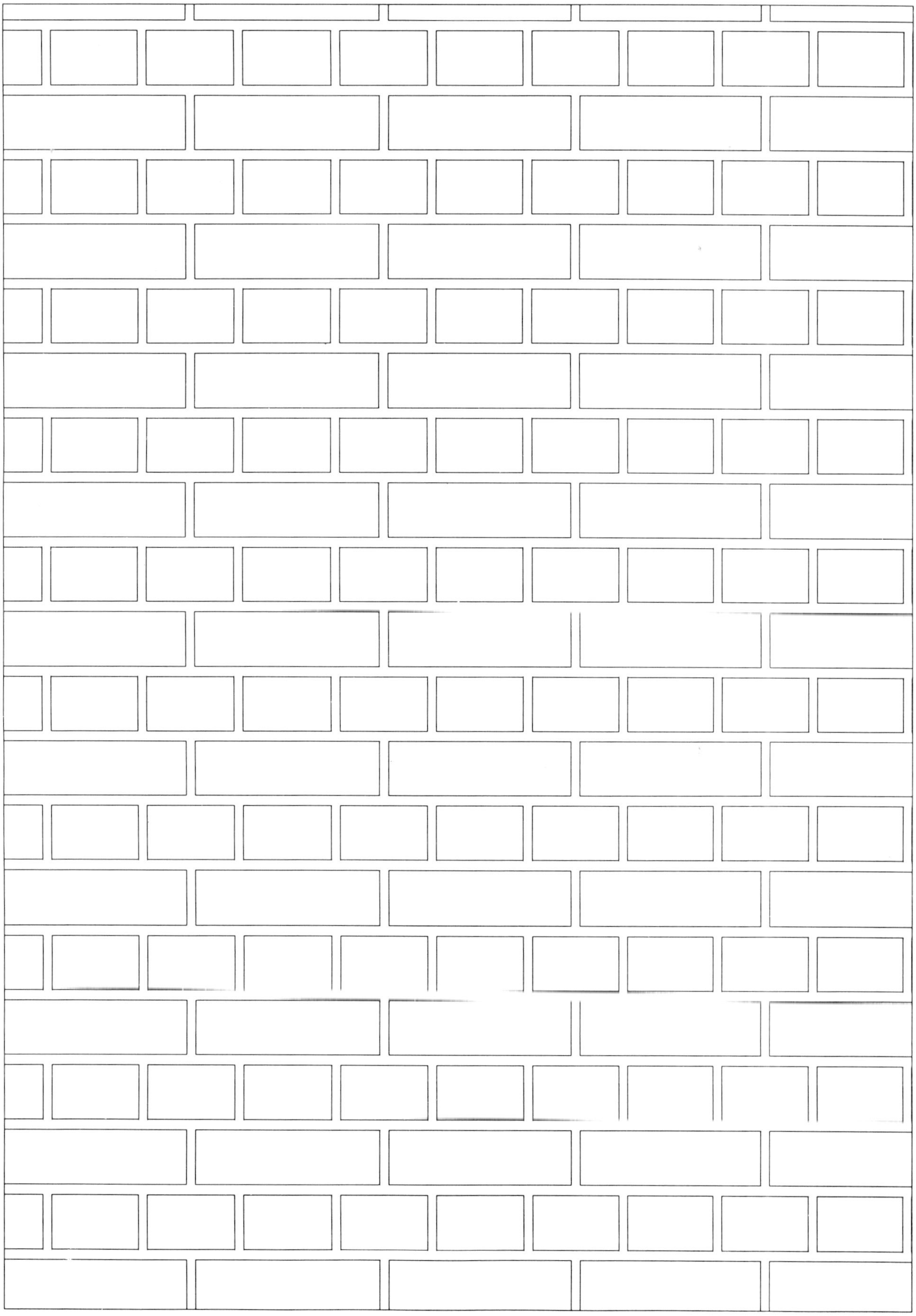

Building materials 4: Small blocks

Building materials 5: Large bricks

Building materials 6: Small bricks

Building materials 7: Large roof tiles

Building materials 8: Small roof tiles

Indian symbols

What do these symbols look like?

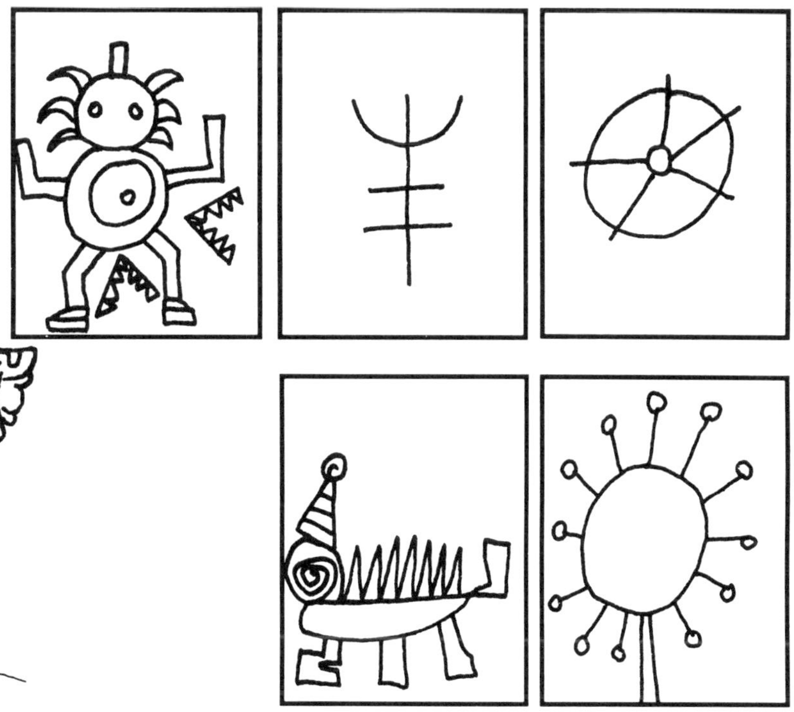

Make up your own designs for the

sun river trees

bear snake buffalo.

Rubbings gallery

Cut out samples from your rubbings and glue them here.

Hard

Soft

Smooth

Rough

Prickly

Velvety

Large weave

Small weave

Canvas grid

Figure shapes

Get some help to cut these figures out.

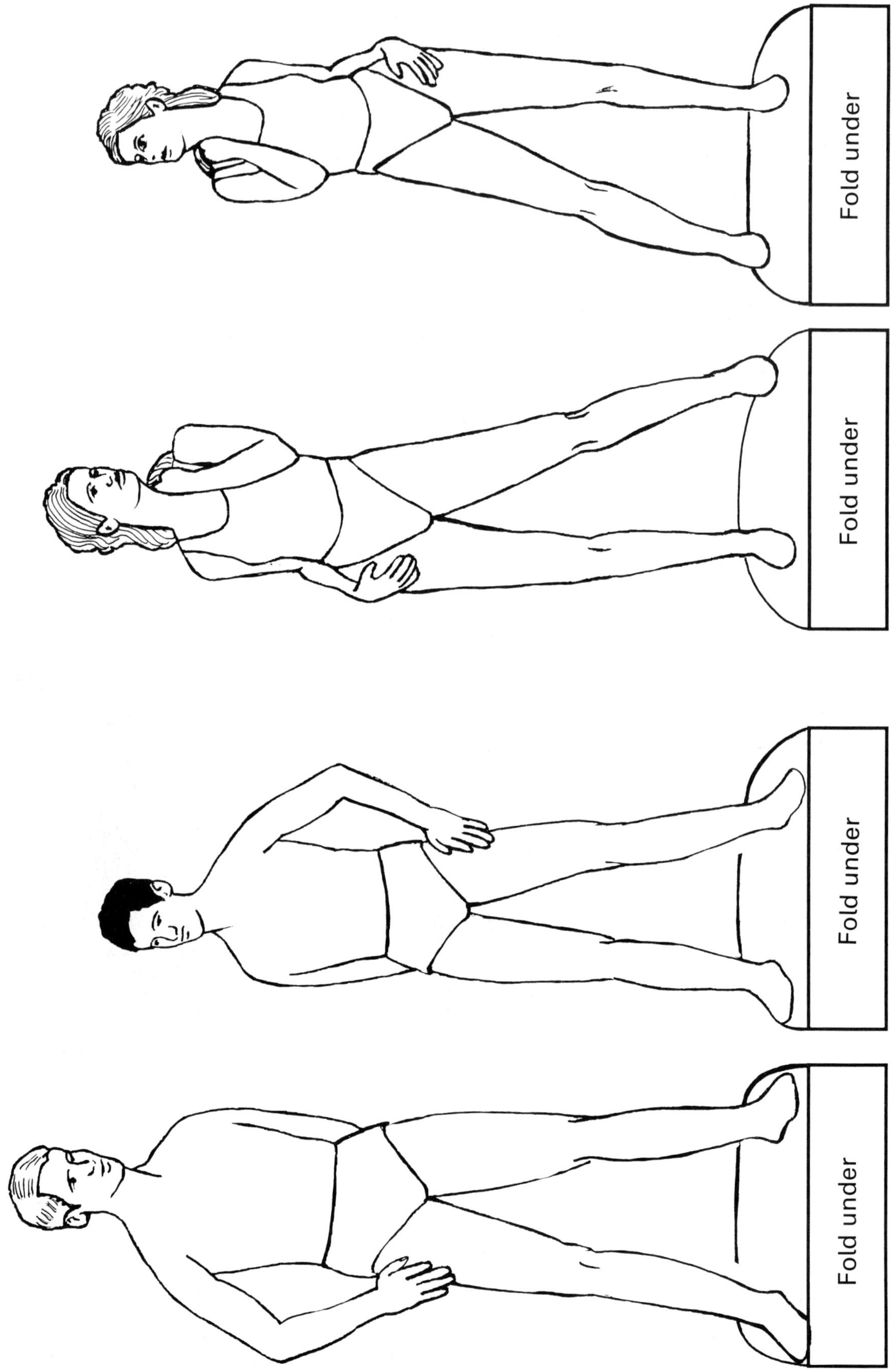

Multi-cultural costumes

Match the words and pictures.

Colour the pictures.

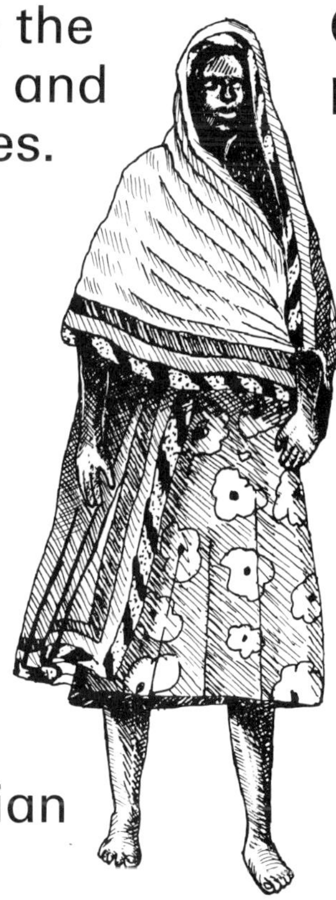

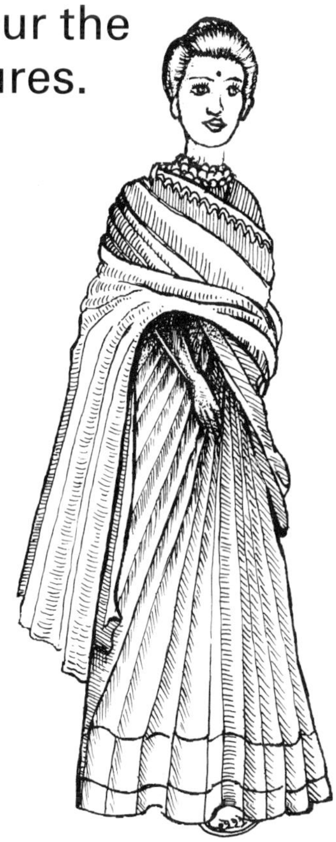

Algerian

Greek

Japanese

Mexican

Indian

African

Hats

Match the words and pictures. Colour the hats.

Turban

Top hat

Mexican

Crown

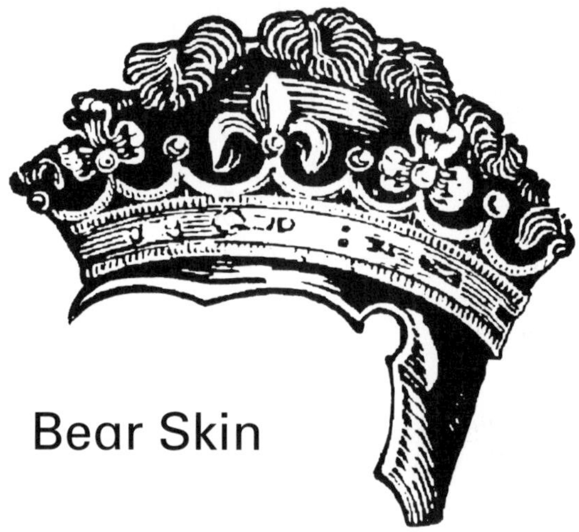

Bear Skin

Chinese

French

Admiral's

Sandals

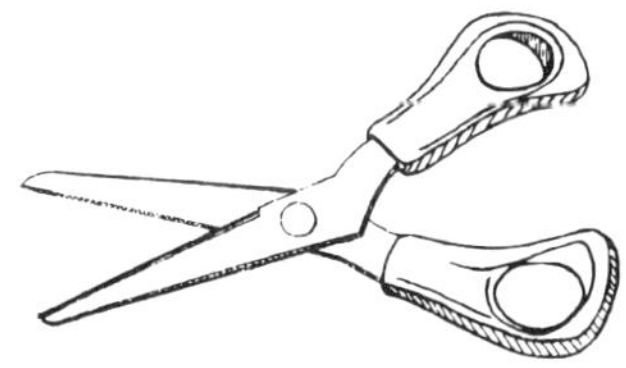

Cut out from card. Cut slots.
Match the numbers on the straps.

Slip straps through slots and glue.

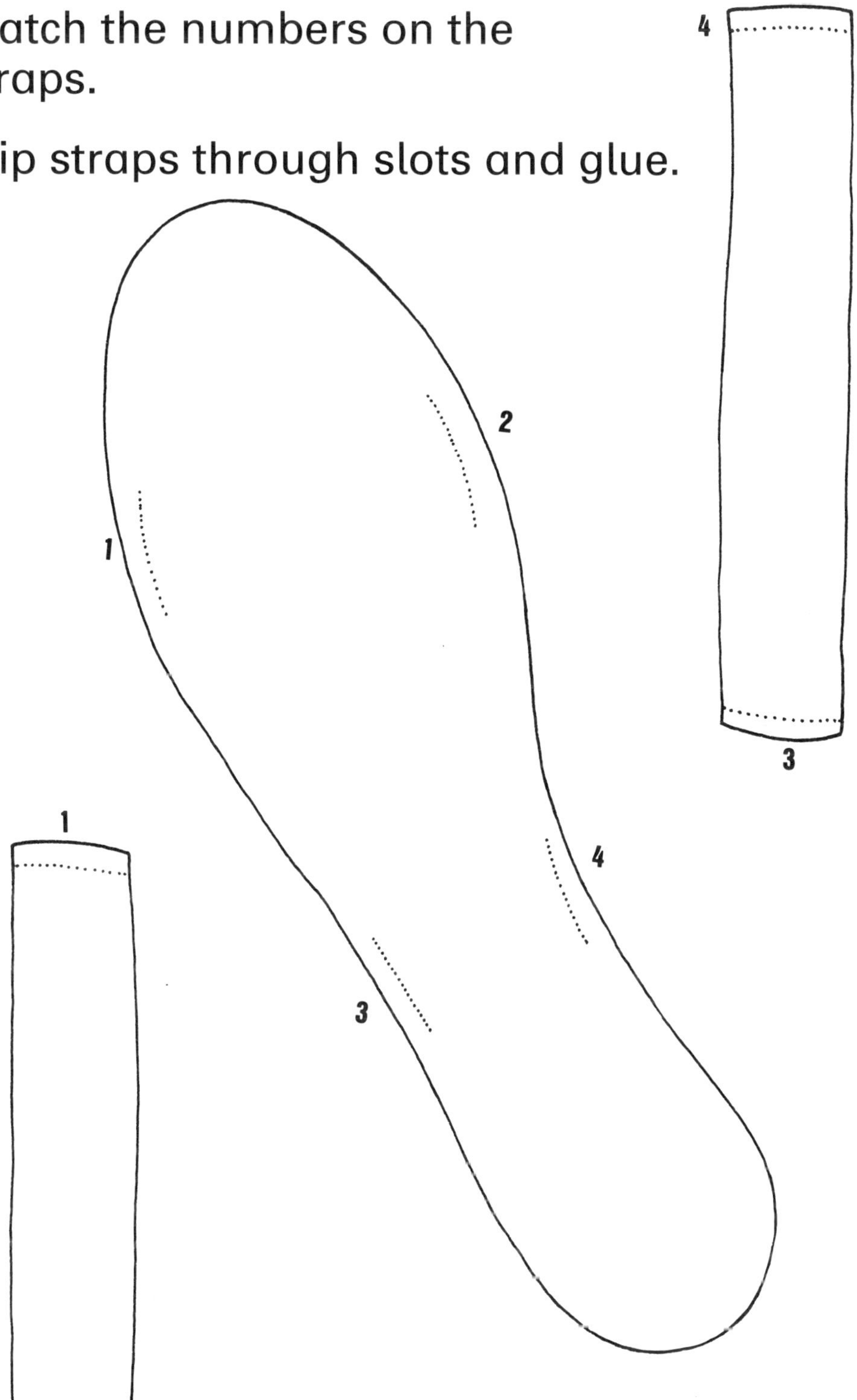

How can you make up the sandal for the right foot?

Clothes shapes 1

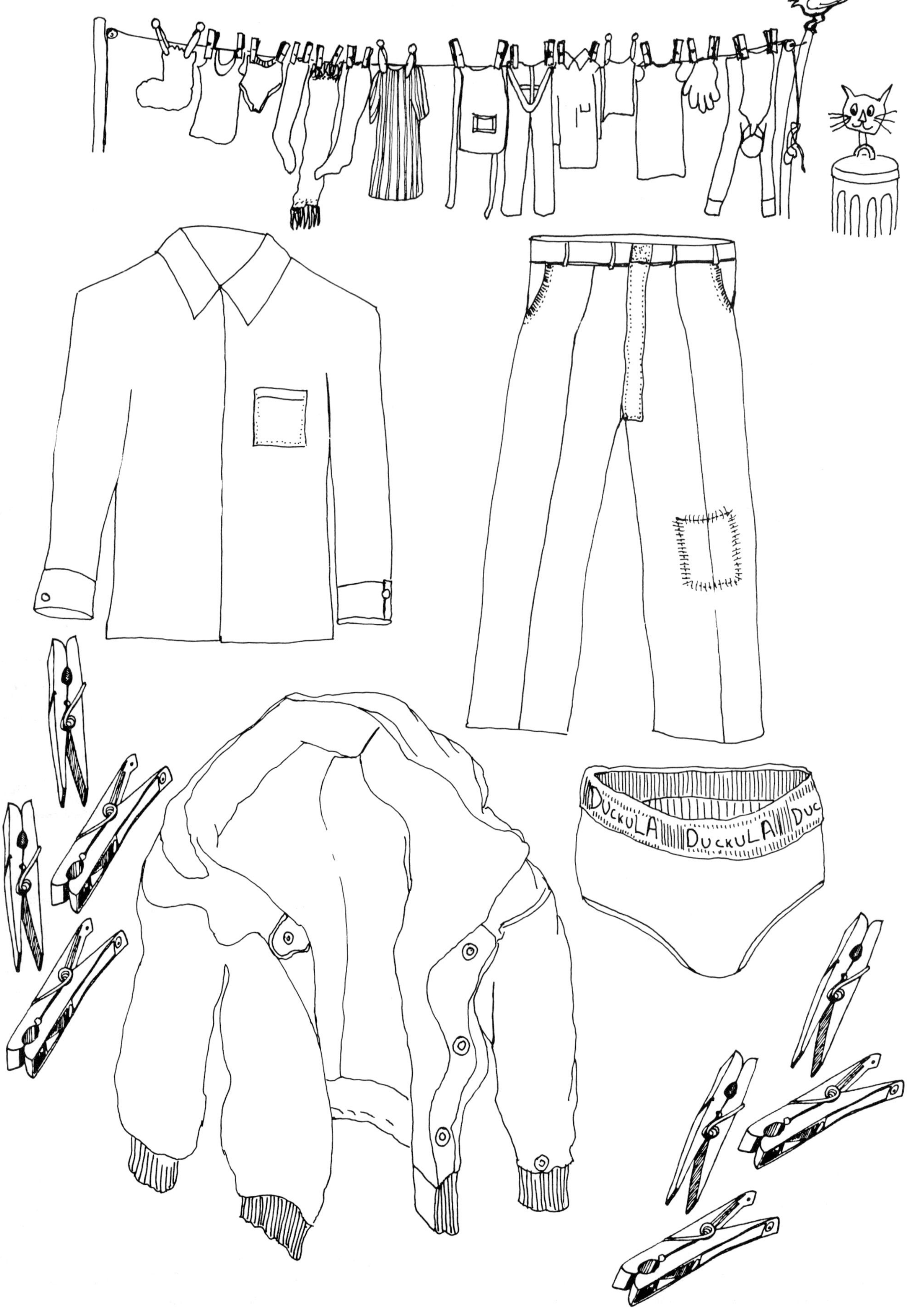

Clothes shapes 2

The Emperor's New Clothes

Show the story in four pictures. Include words.

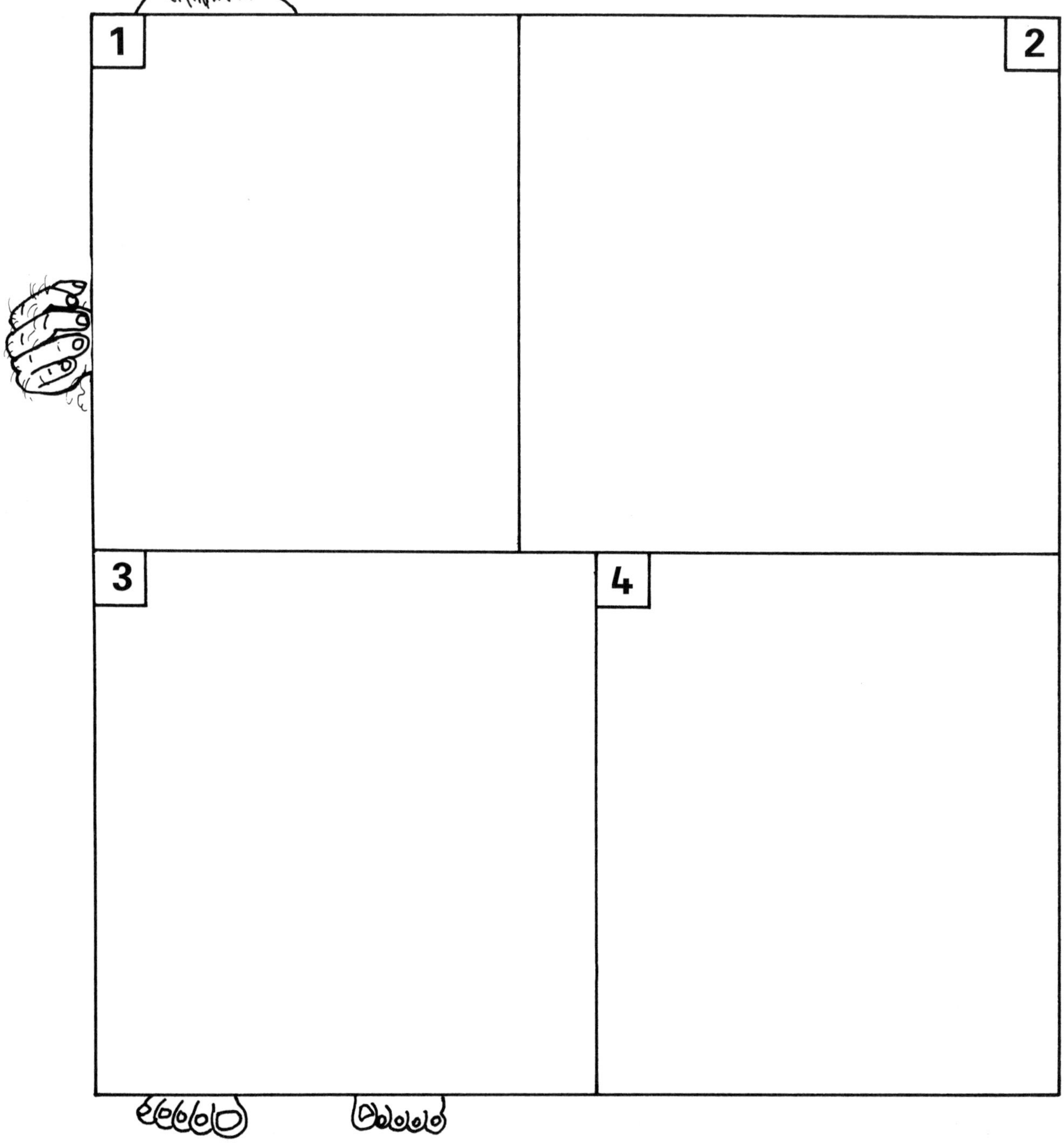

Bag pattern

Cut out from felt. Stitch, fix velcro and the strap.

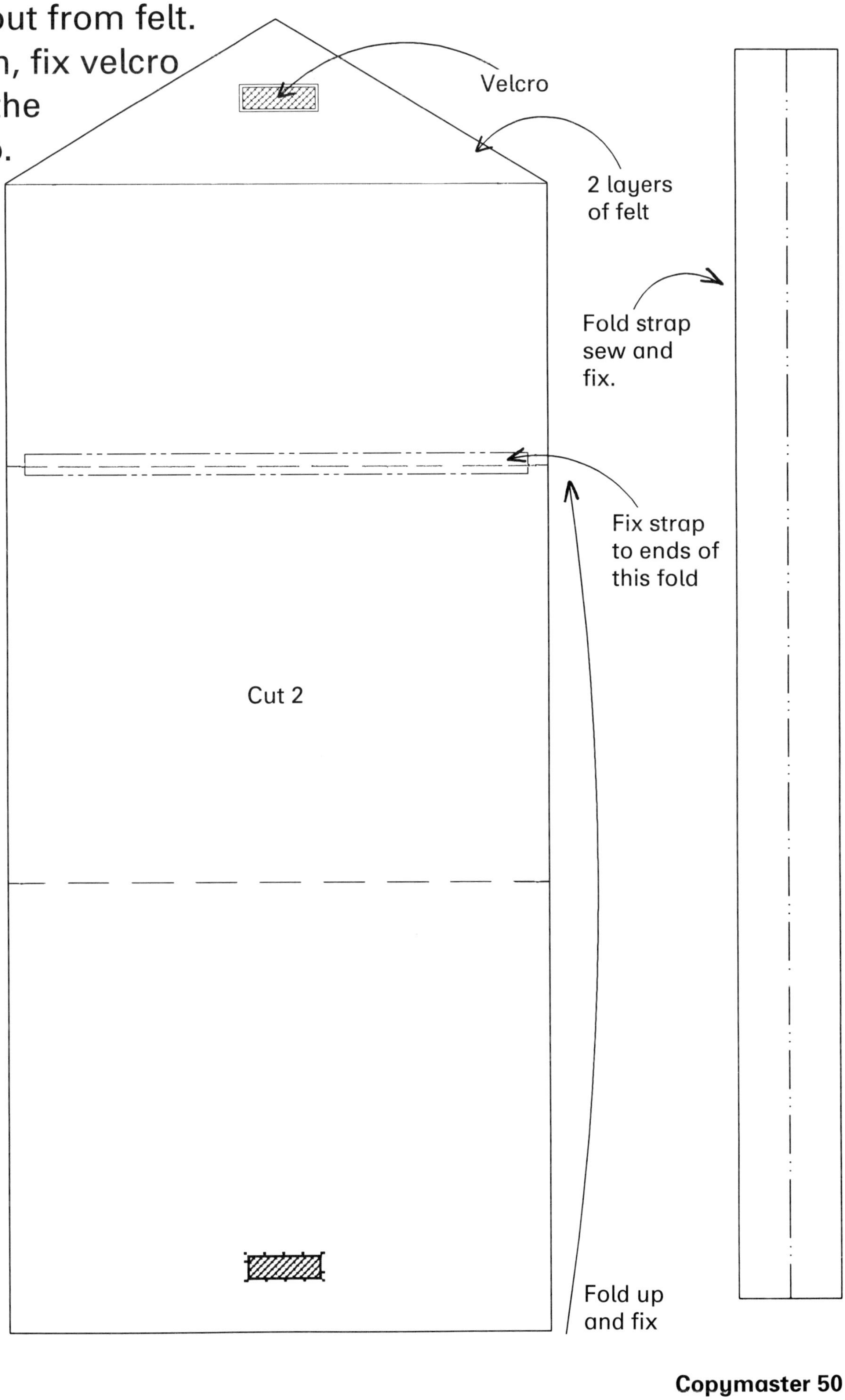

Fish shapes 1

Use as stencils
or for
mobiles

Fish shapes 2

Sea creatures 1

Use as stencils or for mobiles.

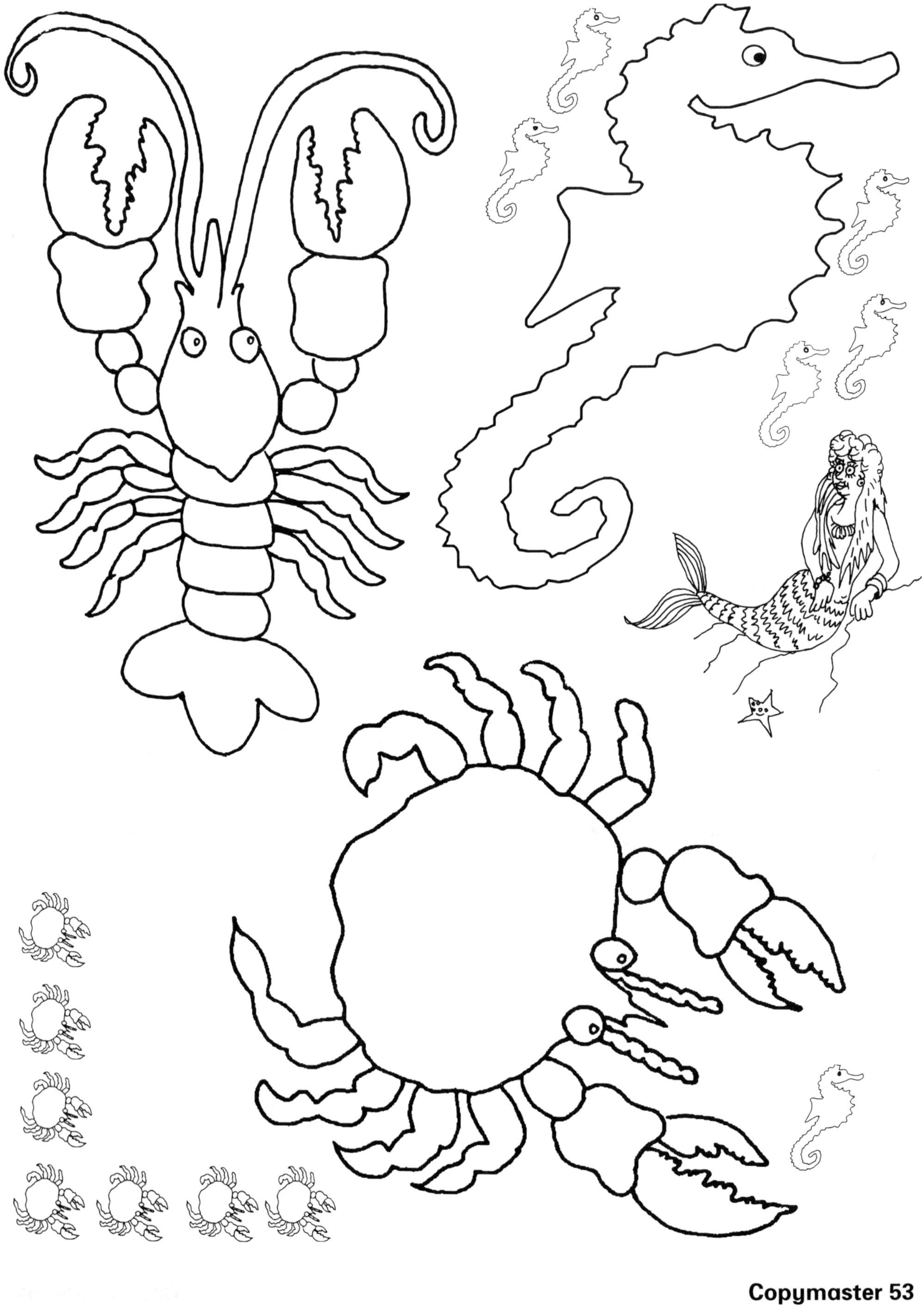

Sea creatures 2

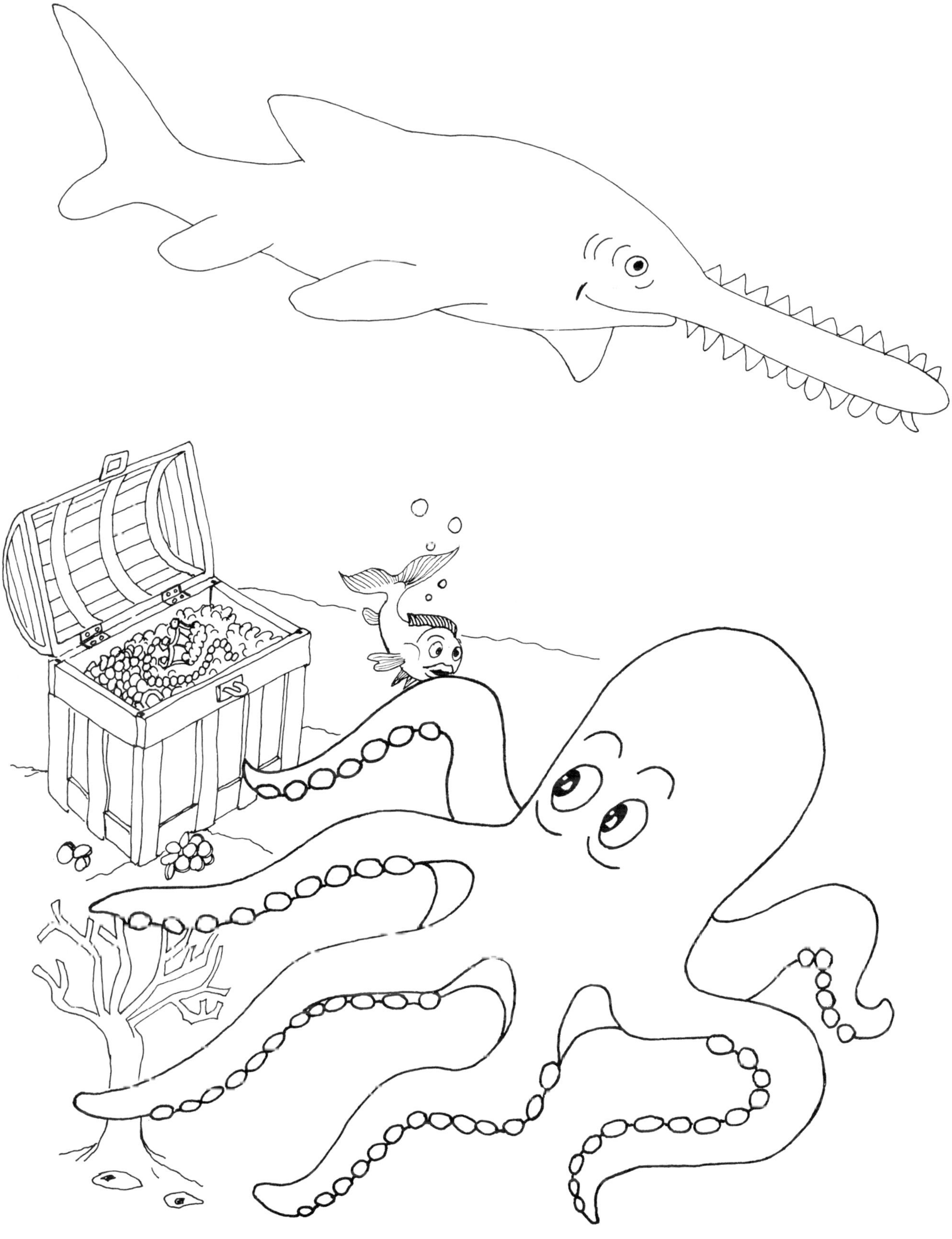

Simple boat net

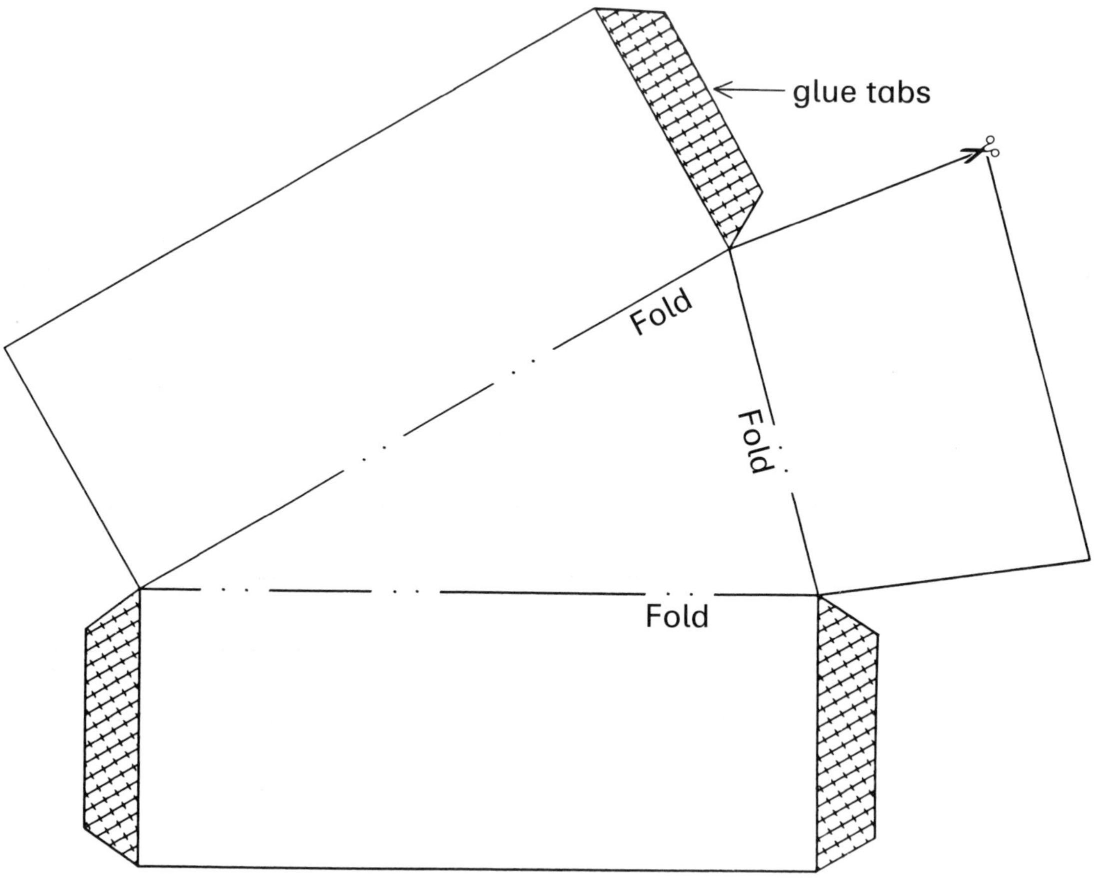

Wave

Cut out carefully. Use as a stencil for making patterns.

Animal shapes 1

Cut out and use as templates, or for stencils or mobiles.

Animal shapes 2

Cut out and use as templates, or for stencils or mobiles.

Animal shapes 3

Cut out and use
as templates, or for
stencils or mobiles.

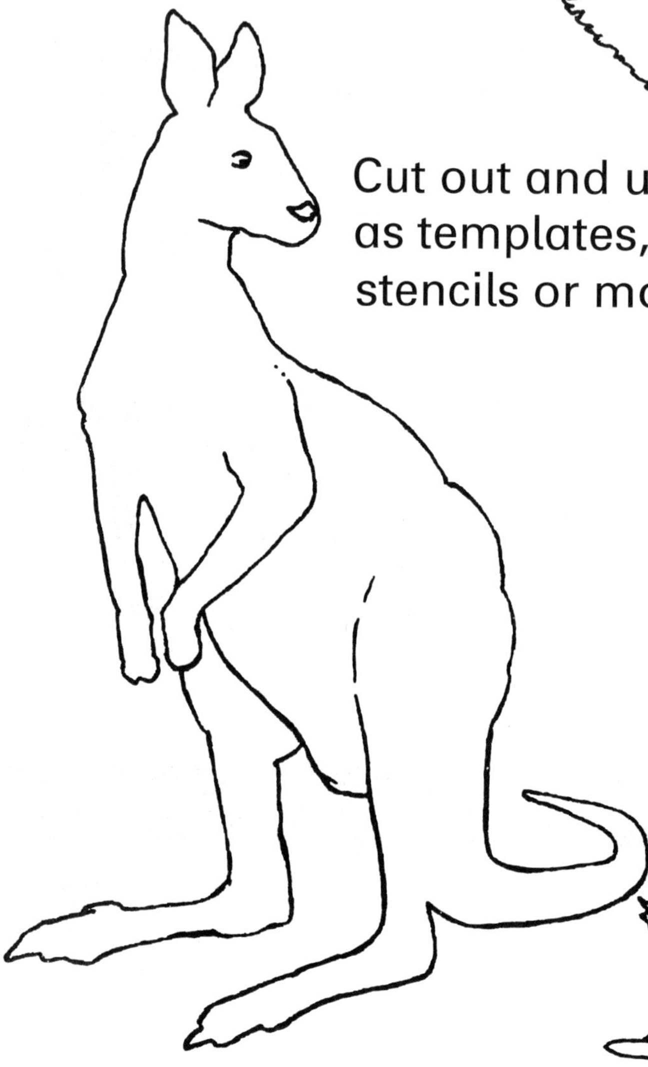

Fancy letters

Use fairground colours and colour in neatly.

Sweet bags and cartons

Use paper.

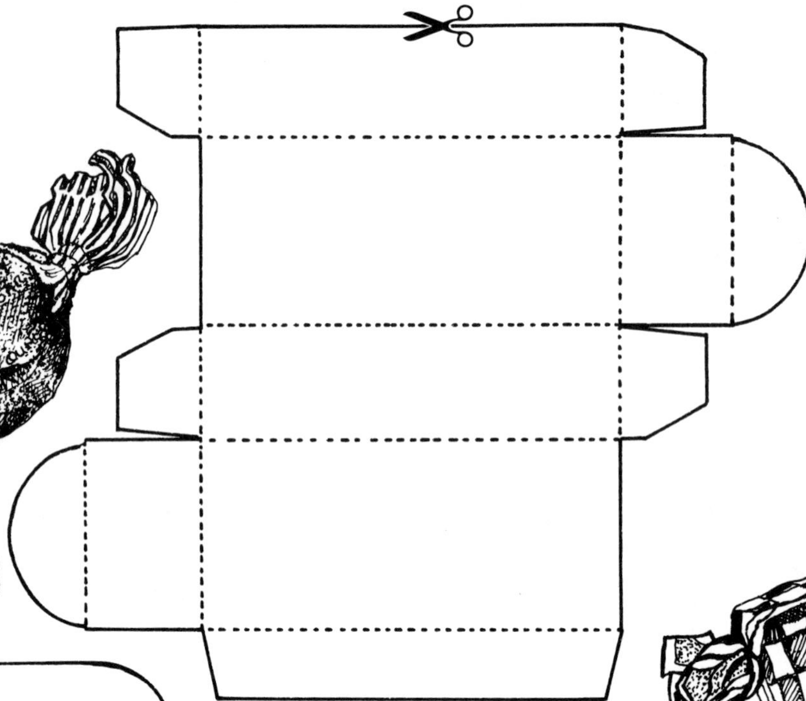

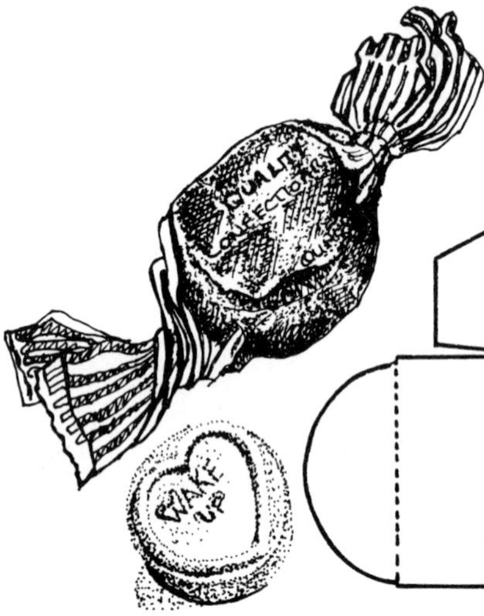

Use thin card.

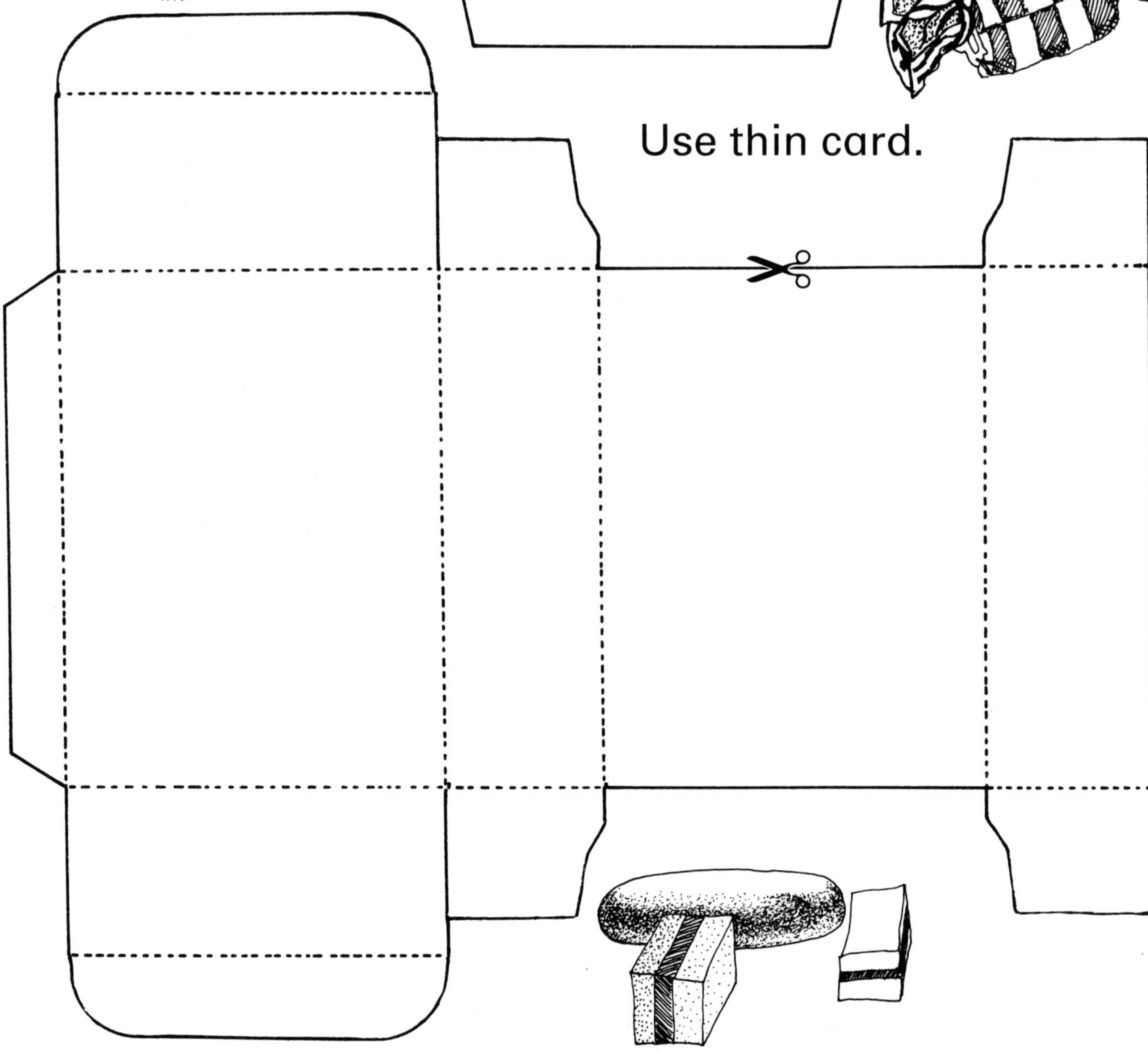

Cut out the shapes from felt and make up a clown's head.

My black and white vehicle

My fantastic, futuristic, moving machine

Hundreds of years ago
a man named Leonardo
designed a helicopter
Can you make a
coloured picture of
your own futuristic
vehicle.

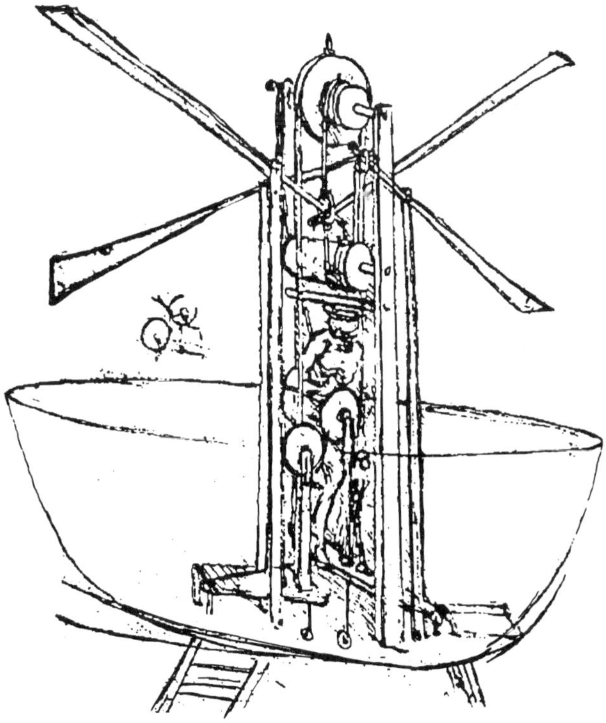

My picture is of a ______________________________

Journey strip map

This map shows a journey between a school and someone's home. Can you make a similar map for your journey. Draw little pictures to show hills, trees, traffic lights, crossings, chip shops and other features.

Lorry net

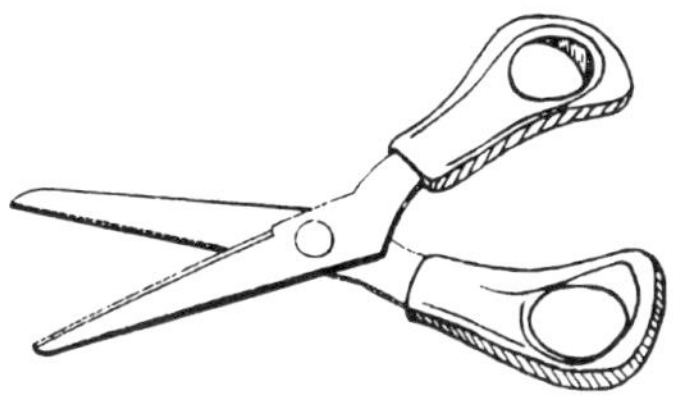

Get some help with this.

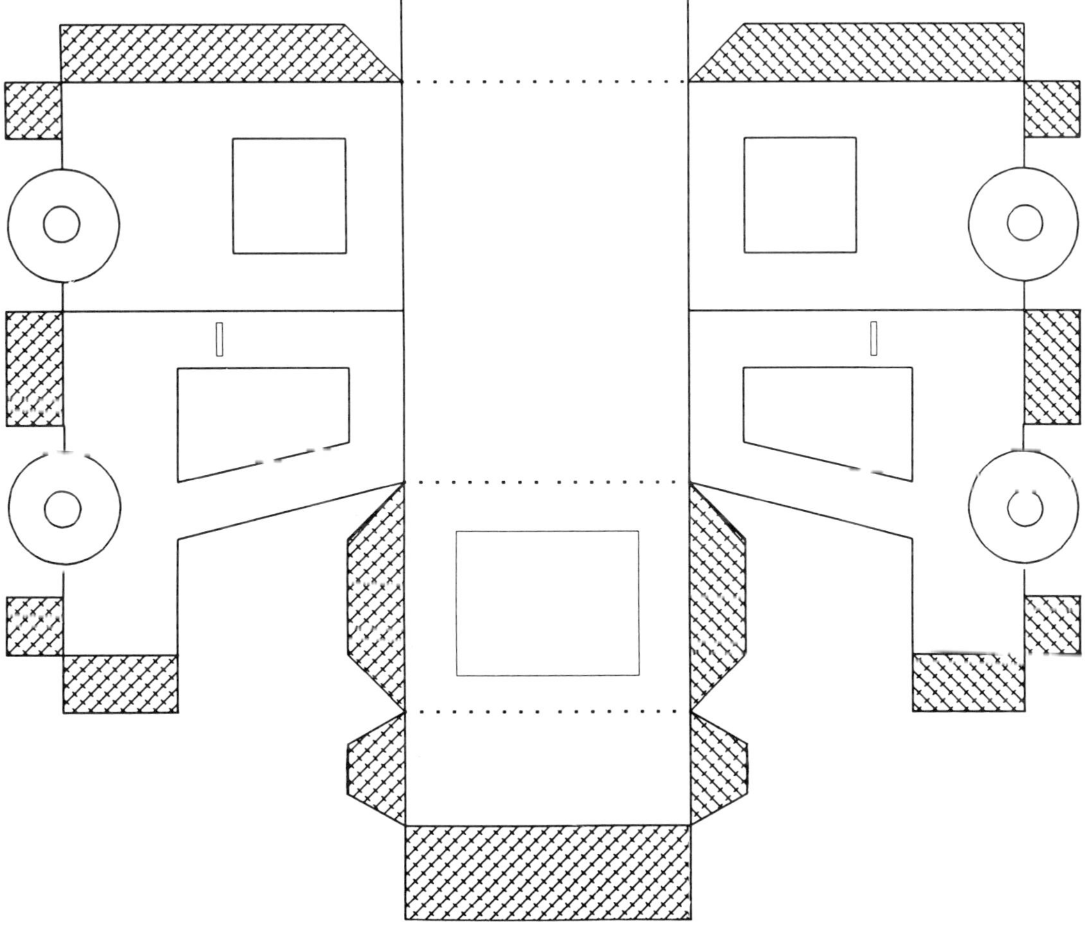

Canal ware stencil 1

Canal ware stencil 2

Simple alphabet 1

ABC

DEF

GHIJ

KLM

Simple alphabet 2

Tree of life

Complete this drawing with your own animals, flowers and fruit.

William Morris 1: Meadow

William Morris 2: Flowers

William Morris 3: Leaf

William Morris 4: Symmetrical animals

Seeds template

Use as stencils for printing borders on fabrics.

Magnify

Do a small drawing here.

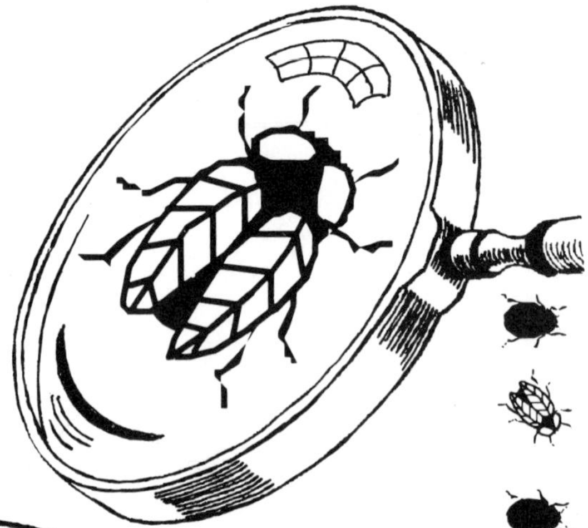

Do a much bigger drawing of the same thing here. Use a magnifying glass.

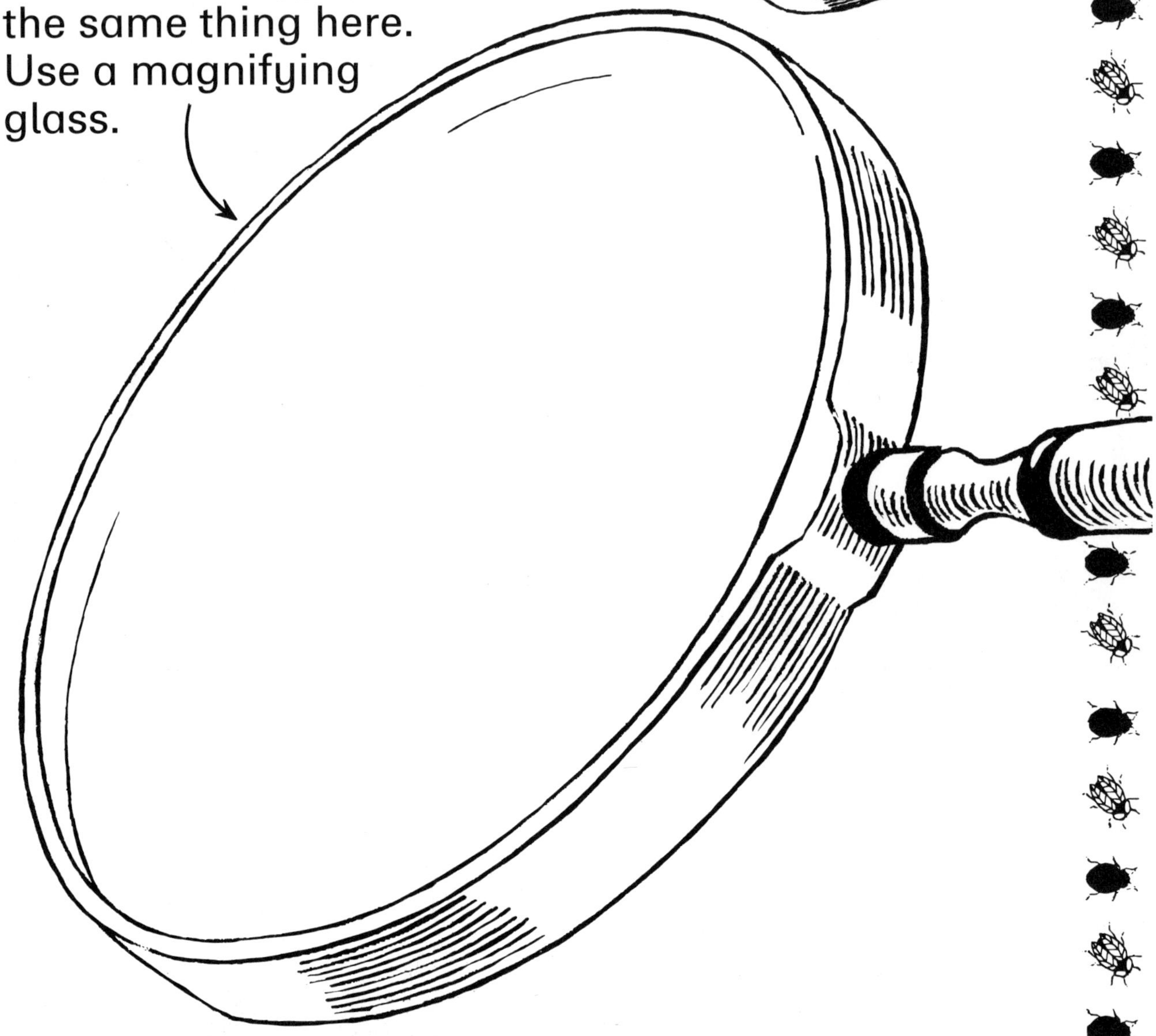

Tangram

Cut out the seven pieces. How many animals can you make?

I can make ________

Simple head

Use this pattern at the same size for making masks or enlarge it by squaring up.

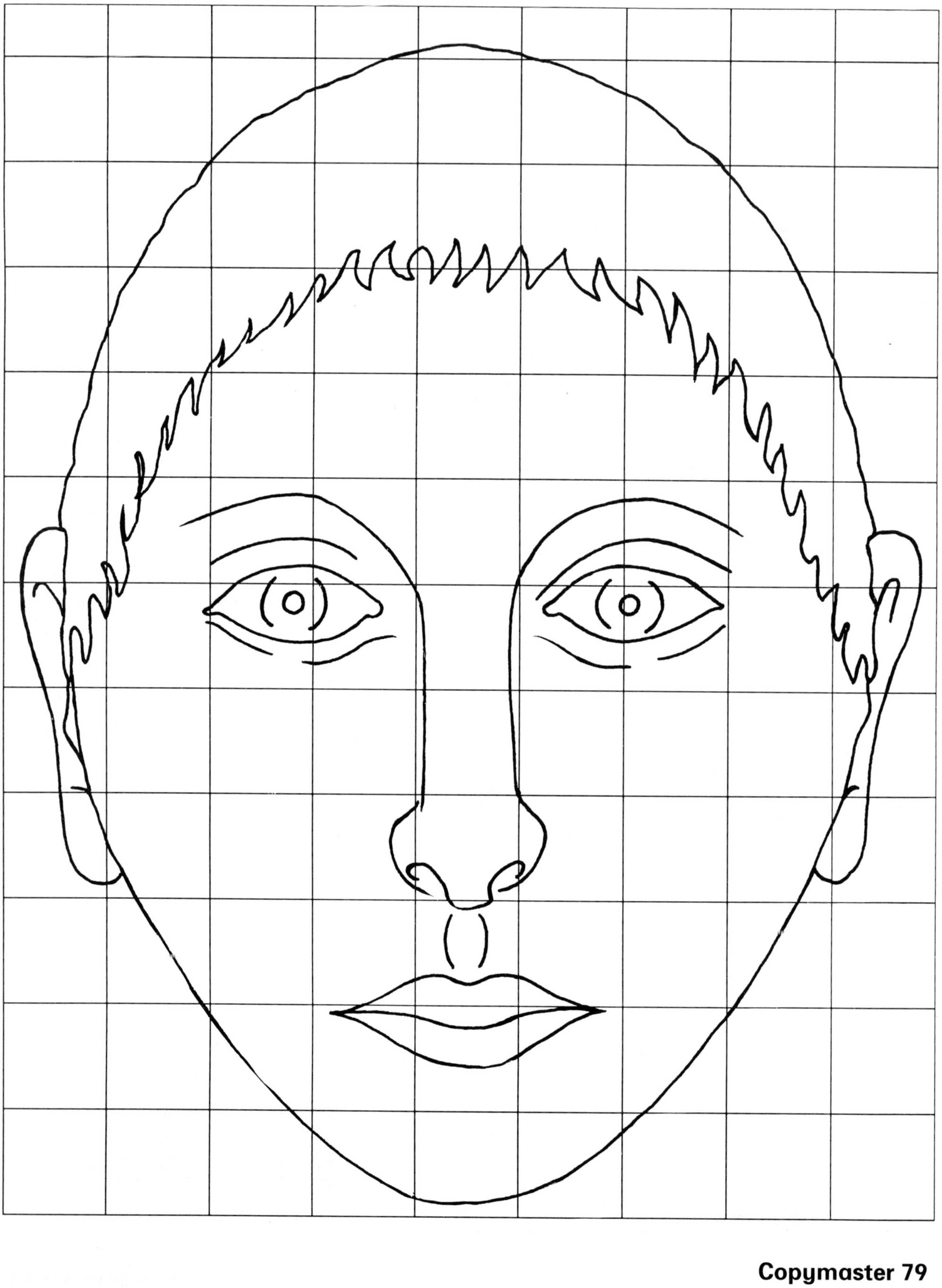

Little dots

Big dots

Colours I have made

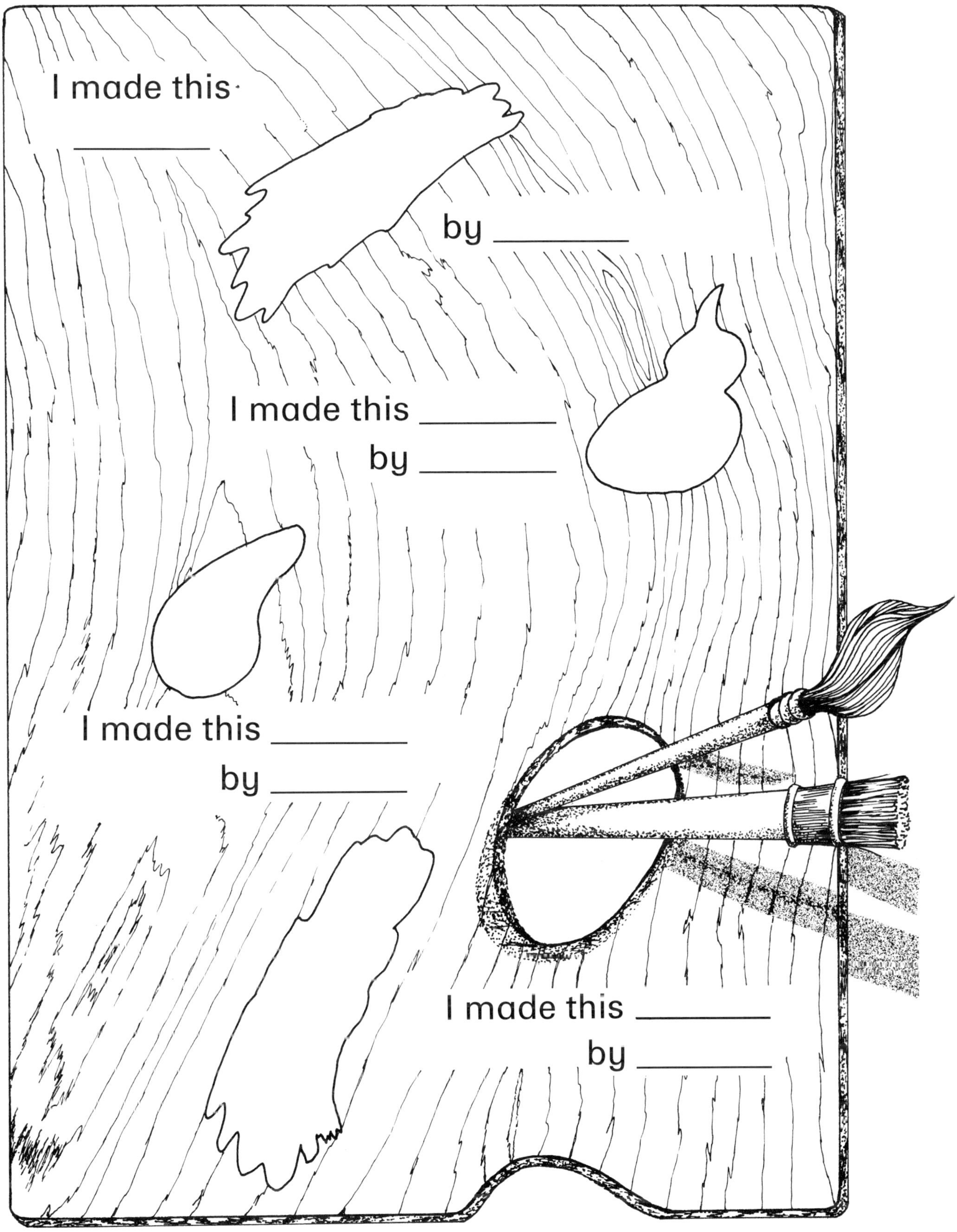

I made this ________ by ________

I made this ________ by ________

I made this ________ by ________

I made this ________ by ________

Colours and shapes 1

Colours and shapes 2

Colours and shapes 3

Colours that go together

First paint the small rectangles with different colours.
Now mix new colours and paint matching colours in the large rectangles.

Colours that clash

First paint the small rectangles
with different colours.
Now mix new colours and
paint clashing colours
in the large rectangles.

Colour spinner

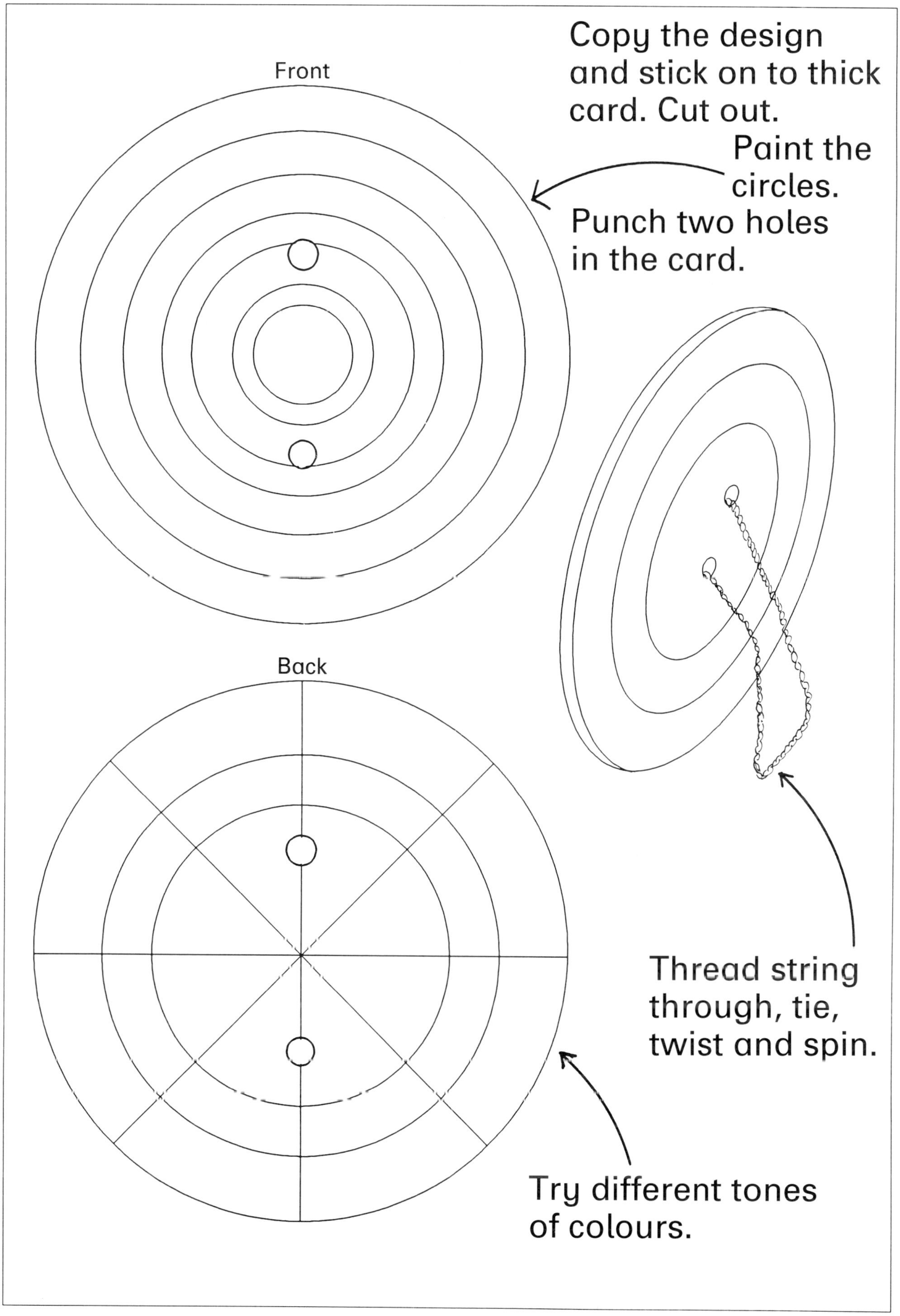

Colour rainbow 1

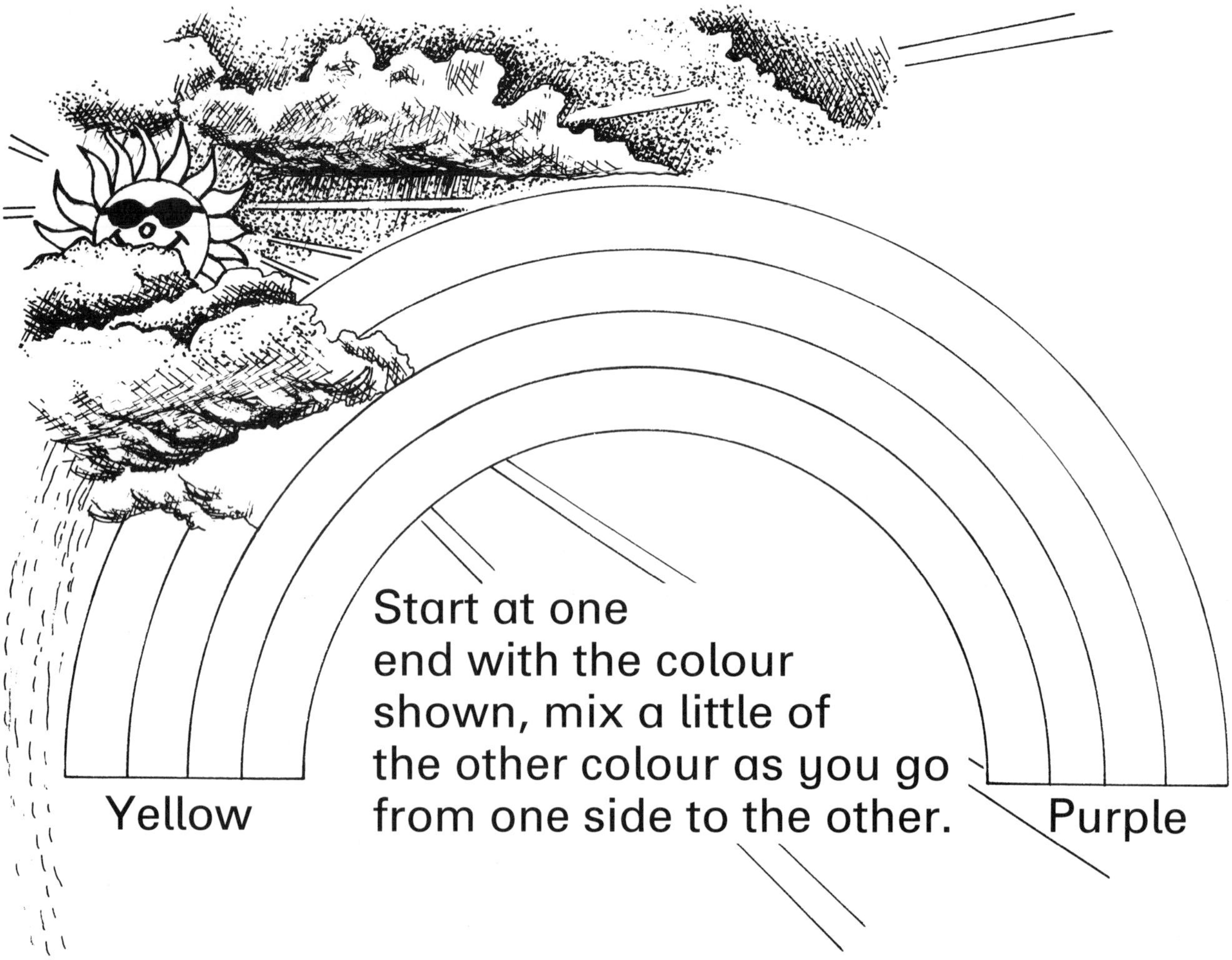

Start at one end with the colour shown, mix a little of the other colour as you go from one side to the other.

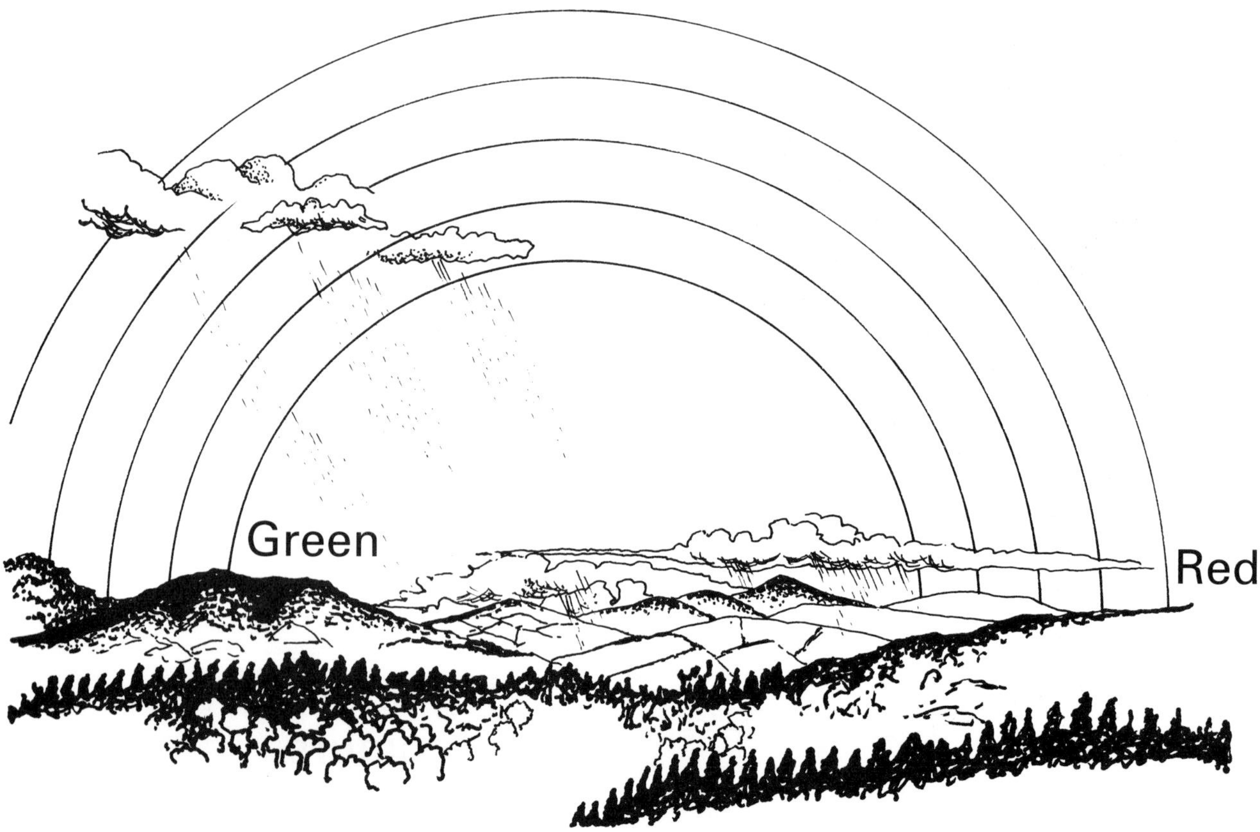

Colour rainbow 2

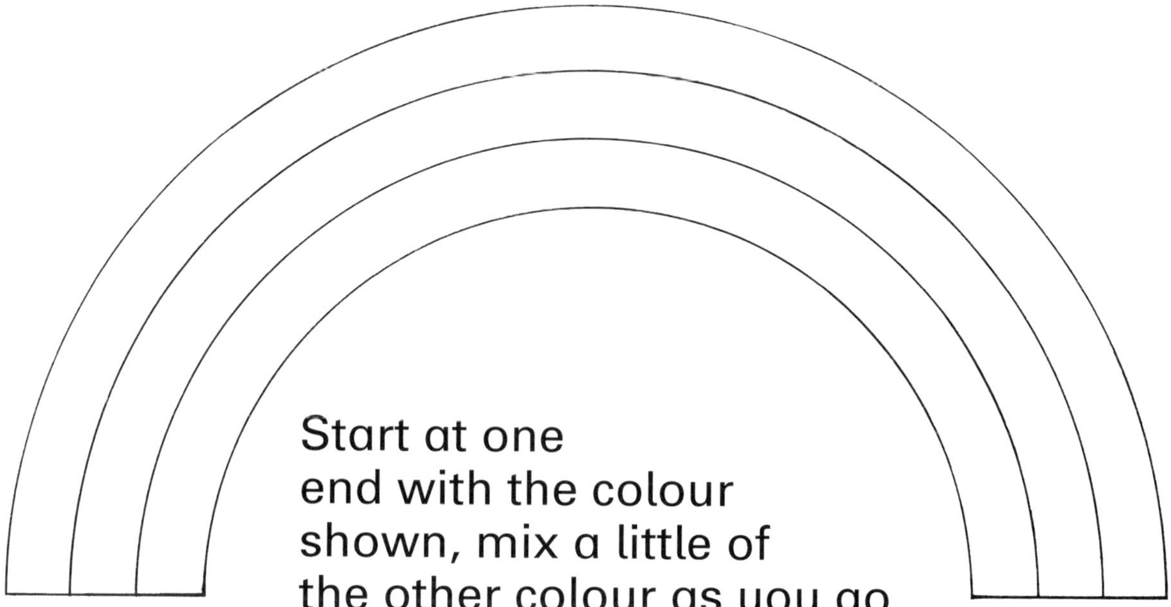

Start at one
end with the colour
shown, mix a little of
the other colour as you go
from one side to the other.

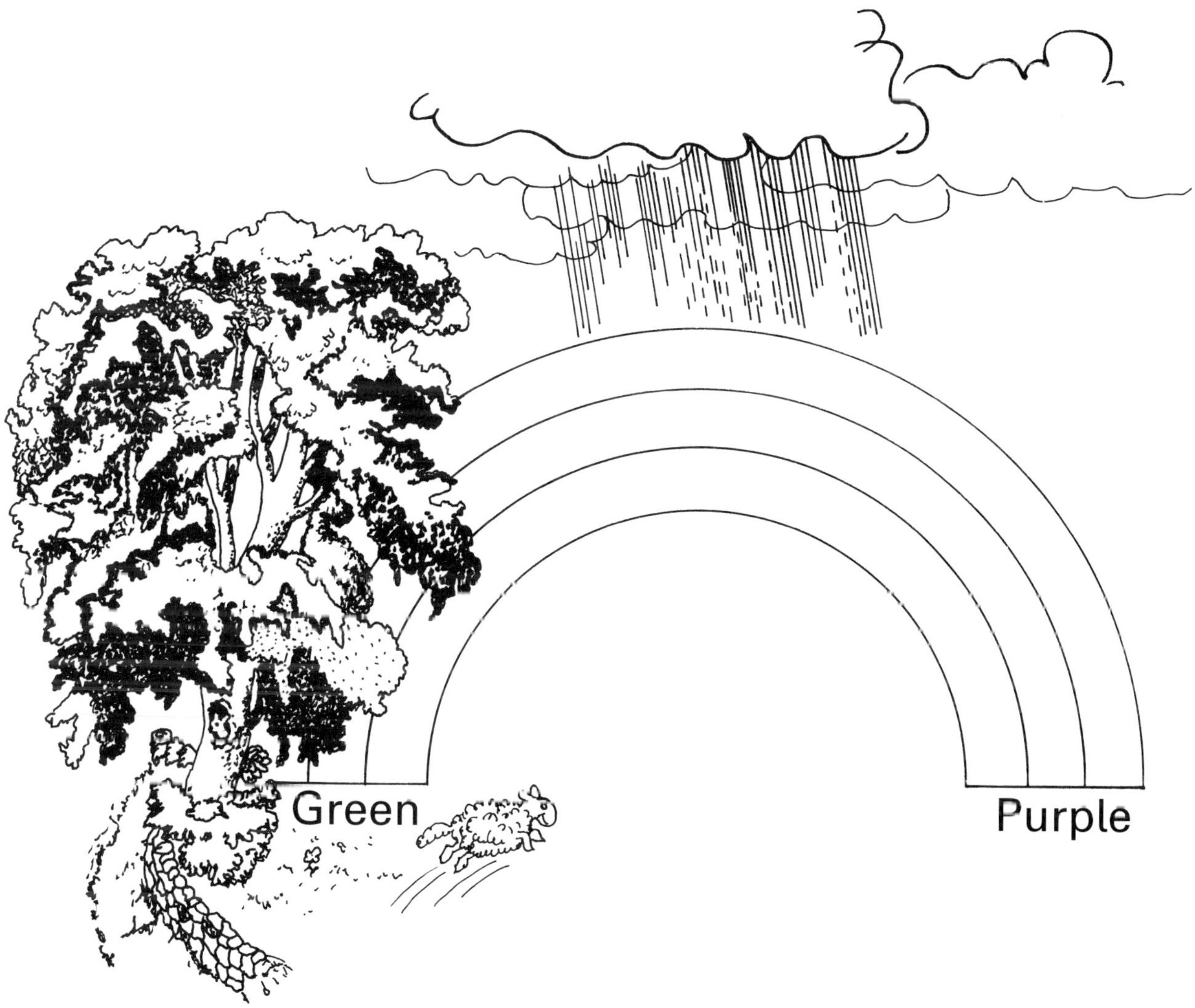

Mood painting 1

How do these people feel? Just use colours to show their feelings.

Mood painting 2

How do these people feel? Just use colours to show their feelings.

Cool and warm

Mix different colours just using some of red, blue, yellow and white. Fill the boxes carefully with hot, warm, medium, cool and cold colours.

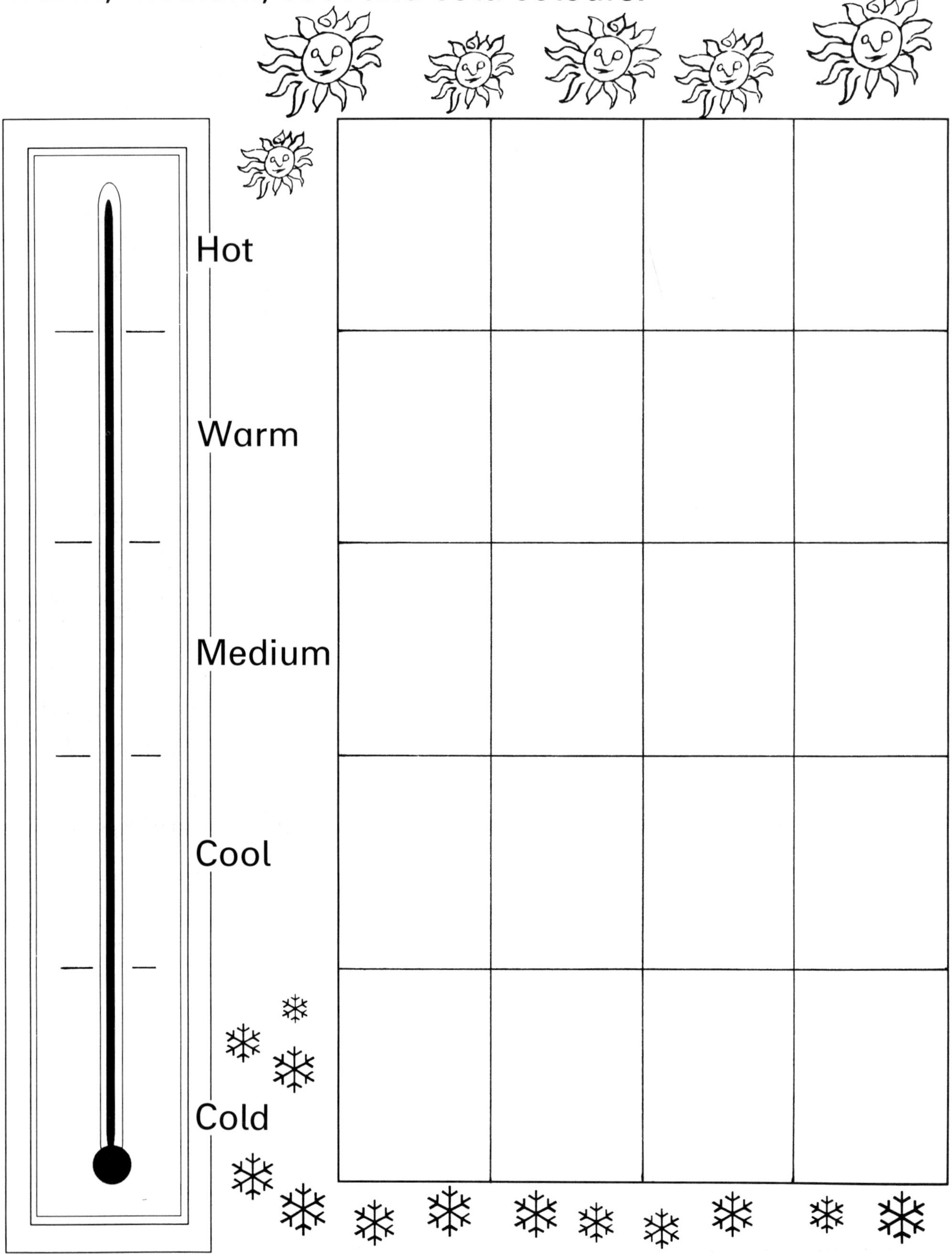

Finger and glove puppets

Cut out the patterns.

Cut out two pieces of felt for each pattern.

Sew along the dotted line and turn inside out.

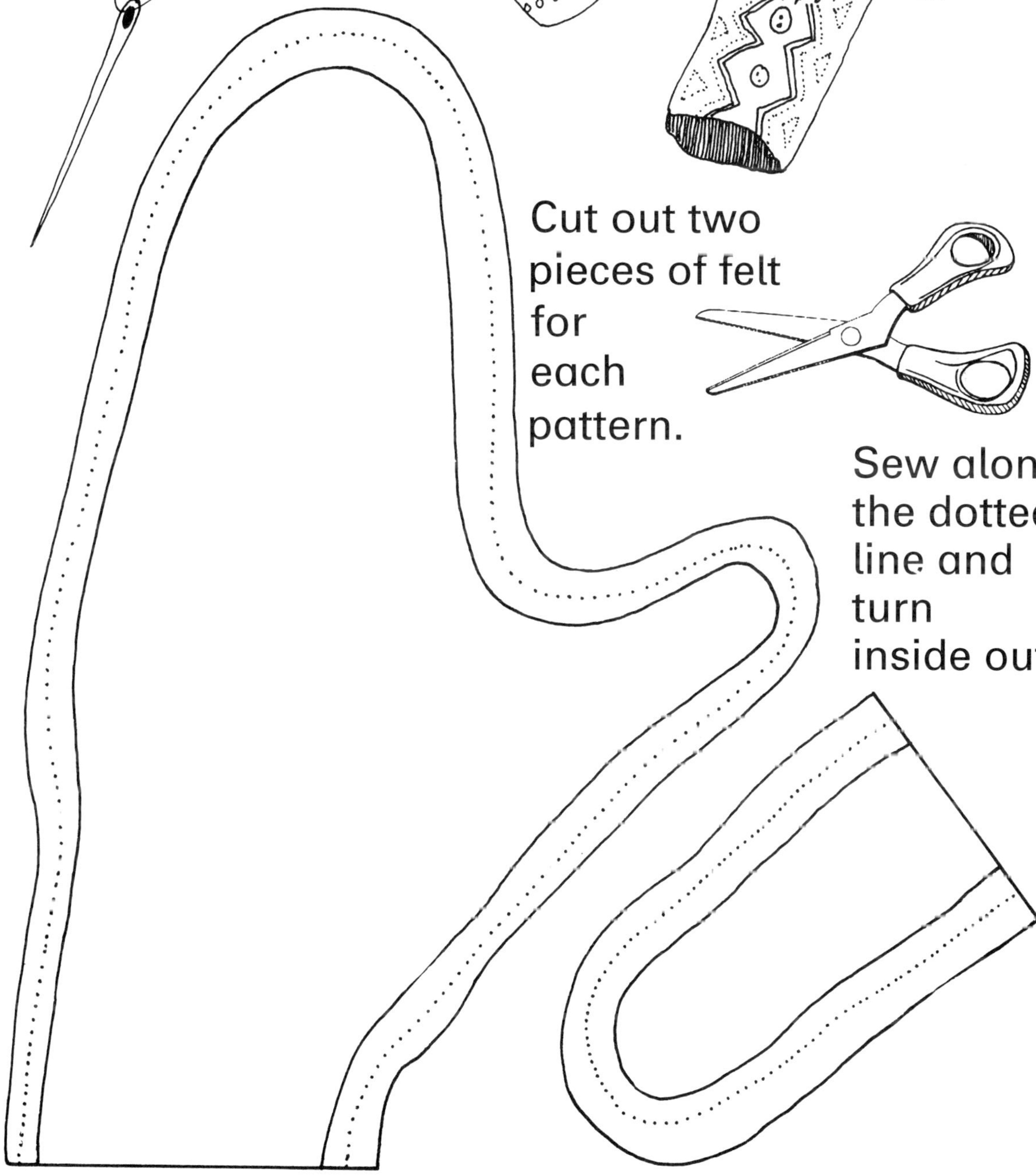

Shadow puppets

Get some help with this.

Trace onto clear, soft plastic with black felt tip. Cut out. Colour in.

Fix the arm and all joints with paper fasteners.

Fix a rod to the centre of the back so that you can hold it.

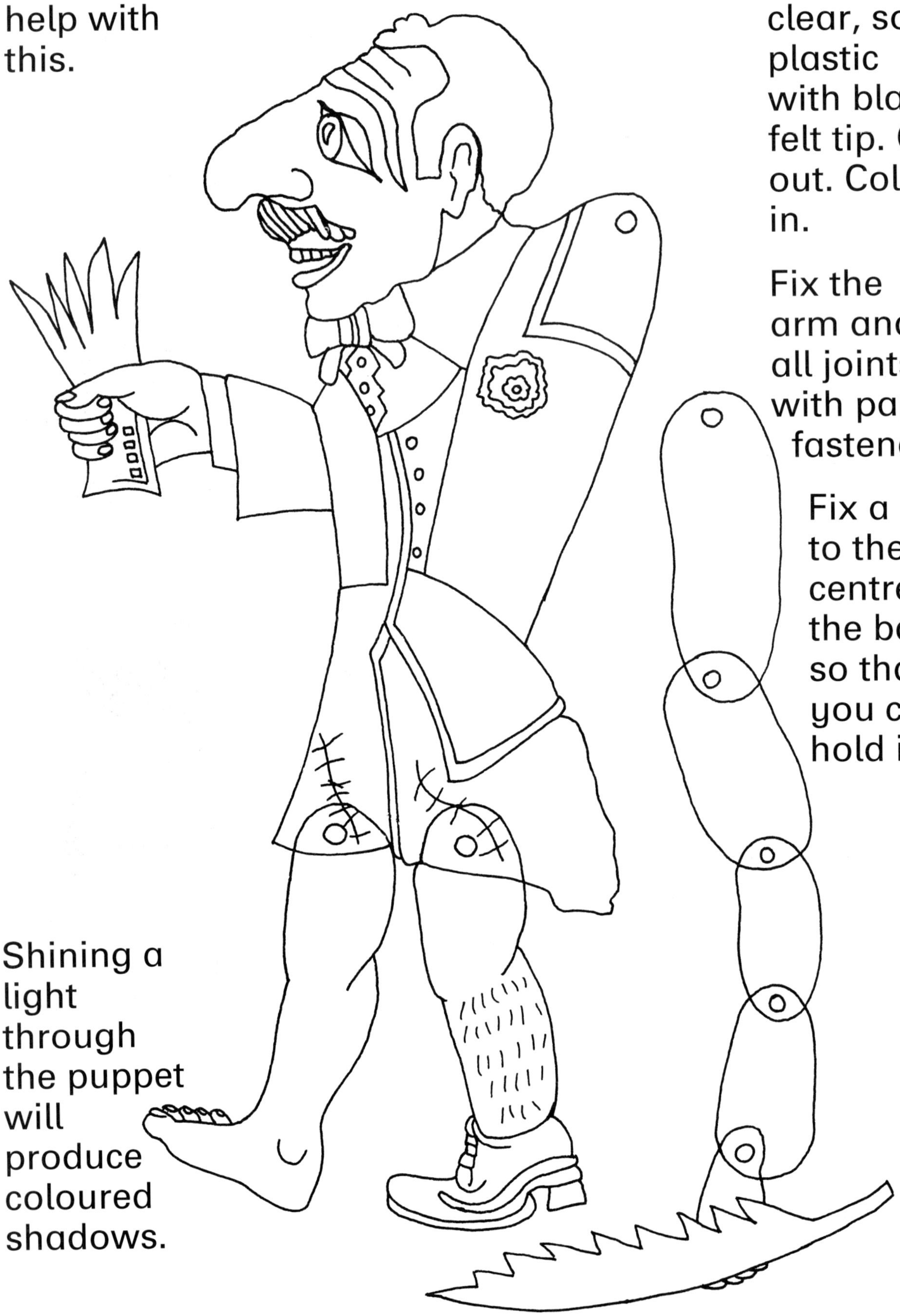

Shining a light through the puppet will produce coloured shadows.

I feel, I remember, I see

1. Feel and draw.

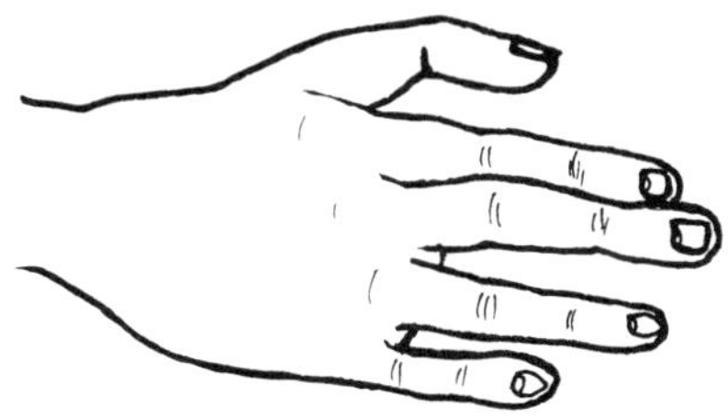

2. Do a drawing of what you remember feeling.

3. Look and draw the same object.

Line drawings of animals and birds

Sculpture quiz

Name the animals.

Which is your favourite and why?

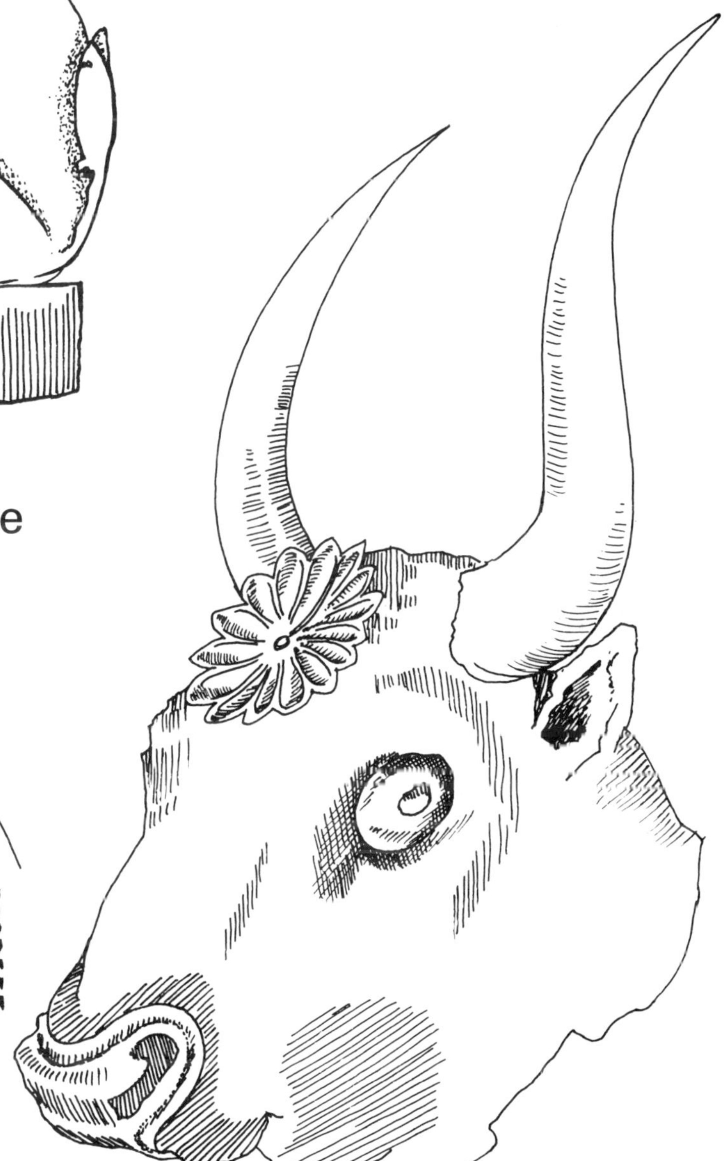

Nets for solids 1

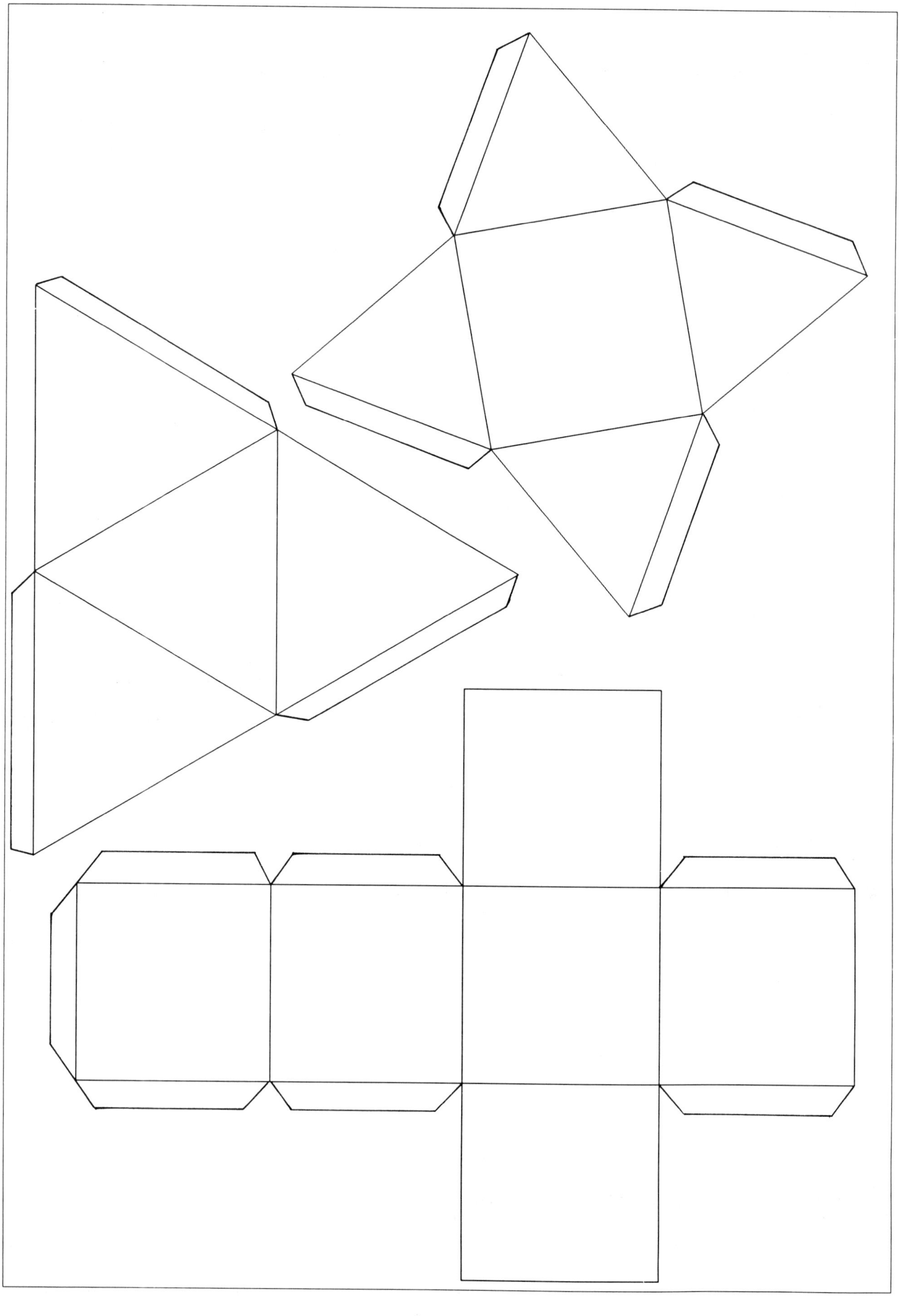

Nets for solids 2

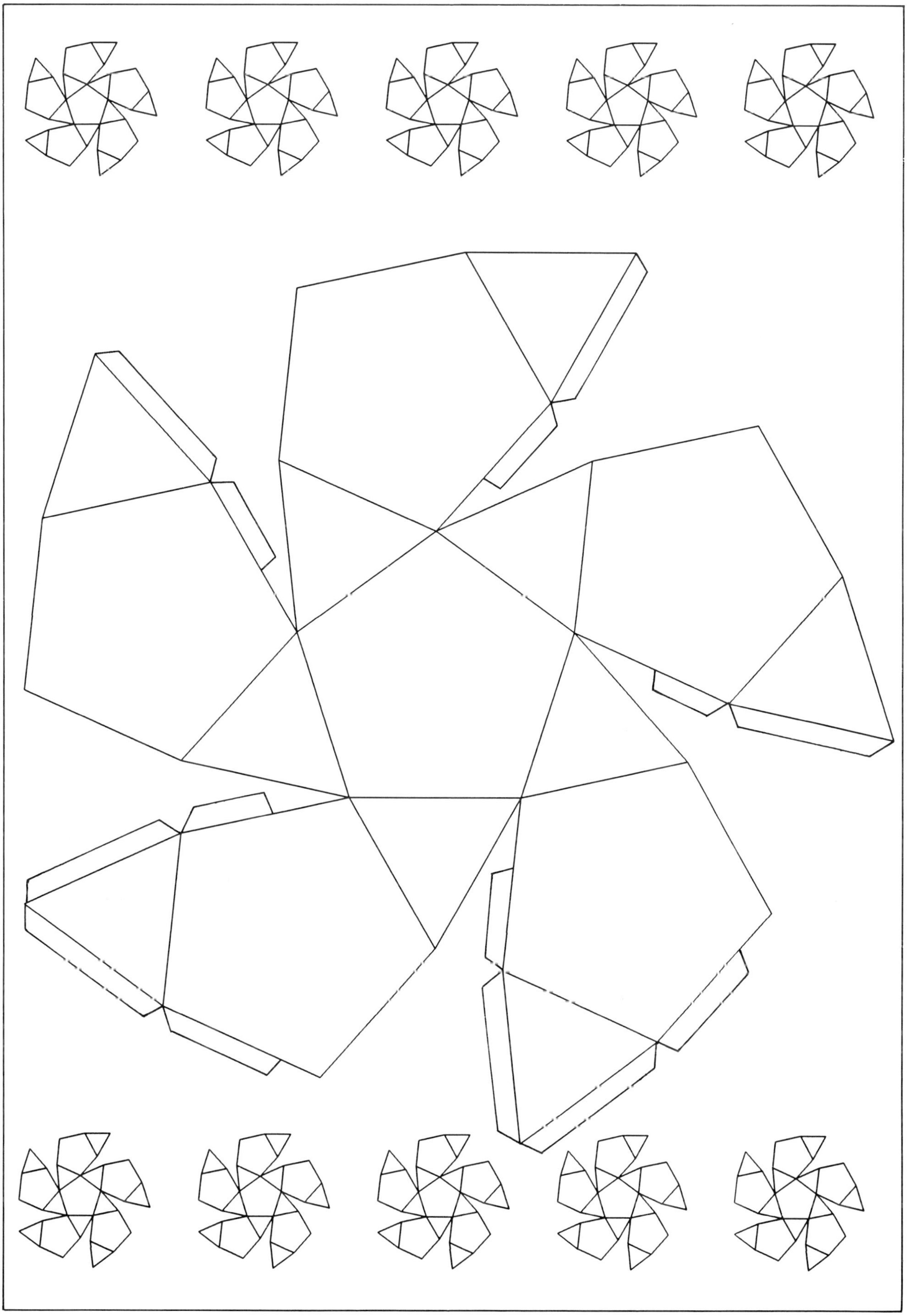

Red and black ceramics

Can you complete the border pattern?

Tone grid

Copy the darkness and lightness of the examples using pencil and then felt tip.

Record assessment sheet

Name	Class	Age	Date		
	A	B	C	D	E
Two-dimensional work From: a) Imagination b) Observation c) Memory					
Three-dimensional work From: a) Imagination b) Observation c) Memory					
Visual Language a) Colour b) Pattern c) Tone d) Line e) Shape f) Scale					
Knowledge and Understanding a) Art history b) Ceramics c) Design d) Drawing e) Modelling f) Painting g) Print-making h) Textiles					
A = Excellent B = Good C = Average D = Fair E = Poor					